MAKE
LOVE
YOUR
RELIGION

HOW TO PUT LOVE FIRST
&
SUCCEED AT DOING WHAT YOU LOVE

DAVID NAZARIO

SDJ PRESS

MAKE LOVE YOUR RELIGION: HOW TO PUT LOVE FIRST &
SUCCEED AT DOING WHAT YOU LOVE

Printed in the United States of America

ISBN: 978-0692087220

Editor: Bruce May
Cover design/layout: Kevin Kauffman
Photographer: Miguel Villagomez, Lost Boys Image House

FIRST EDITION

www.scaredofadayjob.com

ACKNOWLEDGEMENTS

I'd like to dedicate this book to everyone doing their best to make a living doing what they love. And, to those willing to embrace and apply these insights to enhance their lives. Remember, when we are doing what we love, we are doing God's work.

To my family and friends who are like family – Demetrius, Tara, Joey, Teresa, Kim, Hillary, Rochelle, Jamie, Adrian, and the RACC Upward Bound program. I appreciate your unwavering love and support every day of my life. This accomplishment is ours.

To the Nazario and Summers families. Without you there is no me. Let's continue to put love first, no matter what.

To my mom, dad, and brothers. I'm forever grateful and honored to be a part of our circle. Thank you for always being my biggest fans.

To James. This book is what it is because of your guidance and tutelage. I'm blessed to have met you at such an important time in my life. To Bruce, thanks for your expertise and wisdom. Your care and consideration for the written word has been necessary and inspiring. Thank you.

To my hometown and Red Knights past and present. I can only hope that my contributions add to the greatness that is already us.

PREFACE

There's a world that exists where people create joyfully, love ridiculously, and cultivate their passions relentlessly. It is a world that breathes life into itself because it is made of the energy that makes the earth spin on its axis. It is a world anew, that is both of the present and the future, on the horizon of greatness and devoid of mediocrity. It is also void of inauthentic idealism. In this world, open spaces, inviting homes, and warm embraces are felt on a cellular level, both spiritually and scientifically.

In careful recognition of self, love, community, knowledge, and God – in this world – we follow our soul's individual and collective callings as we dance to a unanimous groove. Can you hear it? Can you feel it? It is universally vibrating. Everyone here is doing what they love to do. Work. There are no hierarchical categories because soul callings, as interconnected as they may be, are individual. She teaches. They sing. He sweeps and sanitizes with as much vigor and conviction as any athlete paid to swing a bat or dunk a ball. We paint. He writes. She studies, he nurses, and she CEO's. In this world we don't question ourselves or others about our work because we realize that these assignments were conceived before we were. Birthrights. Whether full or part-time, we do what we love, even when it's tough. We realize that this is the only way to save ourselves. To save each other. To save the world.

It is a world both reimagined and recreated so we find methods to consciously and carefully navigate celebrity and money too. We do this by strategically and meticulously placing love, gently, at the forefront of all of our thoughts, actions, and interactions, and realizing like an illmatically aware and emotionally intelligent teenage King from Queens, that the world is ours. In this world we take risks and nurture our gifts like there is no tomorrow because we realize that the present is all we have. So we take time to be still wherever we are, with whatever we're doing, whether we call it meditation or not. Church. We travel too, both literally and figuratively. We take more trips than we can afford because we know that the energy that is money will always come back to us. And when we can't physically travel, we let our minds transport us until our work ethic and belief in self and God take us to our desired destinations. And finally, in this world there is no fear of the unknown, just questions and answers, understanding and compassion, that continues to etch out pathways to discovering more love. Heaven. Welcome.

*****

When I began writing *Make Love Your Religion*, I wasn't a full-time writer and entrepreneur. I was enrolled in a graduate program at Kutztown University halfheartedly hoping to one day become the director of a non-profit organization. I was in the early stages of figuring out what it meant to be a professional writer. I had not yet begun writing for the newspaper in my city, nor was I in a position to request thousands of dollars to share my insight with a room full of college students. I was content with what I was doing – attending graduate school, working as a college adviser, and writing on the side. I had meager aspirations of working for a big magazine in New York City, but it wasn't anything that I actively pursued with any kind of effort that deserved merit. Then something happened on day eight that changed my life.

It had been more than one whole week since I had eaten any food. The only nutrients I digested came by way of a lemon, cayenne pepper, honey concoction that I devoured incessantly. Mood swings were weaving in and out of my day as they often do when you're hungry, but I was clear. Not only was my mind clear and alert, but there was an overwhelming sense of peace that attached itself to my spirit as an unexpected reward for not eating.

Feeling somewhat ethereal, I sat on the sand colored sofa in my living room and heard God speak to me as the sun poured in through an undraped tall window to the right of me. The voice, which I had never heard in this way before, was God's voice. Not in terms of how it sounded because there was no sound to it, but in its presence and conviction. To put it another way, my conscious was the vessel being used to deliver a message from God to myself. The message came as both a declaration and a confirmation. God told me to use my life to write and help as many people as possible. This was the declaration. The confirmation came almost instantaneously in the form of a text message from someone I hadn't spoken to in years. Seconds after being told what my purpose was, a friend from high school sent me a text message to ask me if she could hire me to write a speech for her. I couldn't believe it. God confirmed to me that I should write for a living and also provided me with an example of how I could use my gift to earn an income seconds later. This was in 2012.

Six years later I can proudly say that I am a full-time writer, speaker, educator, and entrepreneur. I only do what I love, and yet call it work. The pages that follow this preface will give you an exclusive look at some of my journey. My hope is that the stories and experiences that I share, combined with the self-help and workbook aspect of the book will provide you with the motivation and insight that you might need to put love first and create a successful life for yourself according to your individual definition of success.

Make Love Your Religion: How To Put Love First & Succeed at Doing What You Love is a multi-genre narrative that explores what can happen when we choose to put love first and use our God-given talents to make a living doing the activities that we love to do. This is what the book has evolved into after years of writing and not writing. The book that you are holding in your hands is not the book that I originally set out to create. When I began writing around seven years ago, it was with the intent of declaring the Christian religion a detriment to society. That sounds a little dramatic, but it really was that deep. I had had enough of the way that Christianity divided my family into the saved and unsaved, and I was going to do something about it. That's how I was raised. You see something wrong or unjust, you speak up. That's what Harriet Tubman did. My mom loves Harriet Tubman. Almost one decade, many lessons and meditations later, the purpose of this book has shifted drastically. I am no longer concerned with exposing Christianity for what I believe it to be. Writing a book that loves love and inspires readers to do what they love for a living is my priority.

In *The Ageless Wisdom Teaching* by Benjamin Creme of the Share International Foundation, Creme boldly states one of the most glaring problems with organized religion. He writes: "From such simple teachings men have historically constructed complex dogma and ritual, willing to kill and be killed in the name of their ideology. Such religious intolerance has been, and continues to be, the basis for much of the discord and suffering in the world." Like Creme I believe that religion has complicated many of life's simplest teachings in pursuit of declaring one ideology more *right* than the other. Despite this, above all the doctrine, science and research, there is one theme that remains constant in all religions. That theme is love. It continues to serve as the nucleus for all of the world's major religions because there is no truth that is as absolute as love.

On our best and worst days we are love. When we make decisions, whether they be rooted in loneliness, goodwill or anger, we are ultimately longing for some form of love. The world needs more it. On many days acknowledging that the world needs more love has been my source of inspiration when writing this book presented itself as a mountain impossible for me to climb.

CONTENTS

INTRODUCTION

Message In The Music:

"What's Going On"
by
Marvin Gaye

"You know we've got to find a way
To bring some lovin'
here today."

MAKE LOVE YOUR RELIGION

HOW TO PUT LOVE FIRST

Beyond this introduction there are six chapters. Each chapter was picked for a specific reason and the chapter order is on purpose as well. After the introduction we move to the Love Of Self chapter. This chapter is first because it all starts and ends with us, not from an egotistical or anti-God perspective, but from a place of realizing that we have the divine spirit of the ultimate Source within us. So much of what I have been taught and what is taught in the Western world has been used to indoctrinate us with the idea of looking for a God outside of self. This is why we are starting the book with the Love Of Self chapter. By putting the Love Of Self chapter first I am not placing self over God, I'm actually doing the opposite. There is no completely honest recognizing self without recognizing the God within. This is a large part of what the Love Of Self chapter is about. By starting with the Love Of Self chapter and ending with the Love of God chapter we start by focusing on the God within, and end the book with a focus on God externally; both are important. Among other topics in this chapter, we'll explore how to follow our unique paths, the importance of doing our best, and why it is valuable for each of us to have a morning ritual.

Next is the Love Of Community chapter. After we explore Love Of Self, we have to figure out how to share this love. This is what the Love Of Community chapter is about. We'll explore ways to mindfully contribute to the spaces we inhabit, and discover why helping others is ultimately the best way to help ourselves.

After this is the Love Of Knowledge chapter. In the Love of Knowledge chapter I write about topics like: yoga, meditation, church, and the afterlife, in an attempt to shed light on how each of these areas can assist us with putting love first and using our God-given talents to succeed at doing what we love for a living.

The Love Of Celebrity Life chapter is next. This chapter is not about money or wealth at all, which is why I placed it before the Love Of Money chapter. The Love of Celebrity Life chapter is not about being famous either. When I'm suggesting that you live a "celebrity life" I'm encouraging you to adopt behaviors like: working hard, eating the best and most nutritious foods, being charitable, making health and wellness a priority, traveling, and living abundantly, based on your own definition of abundance. This is what having a Love Of Celebrity Life is about.

We then we move on to the Love Of Money chapter. The Love Of Money chapter is about being aware of limiting thoughts, attitudes, and actions that may be stunting our economic growth. So we'll take a look at why we should take more trips than we can "afford," as well as how gratitude is the key to accumulating monetary and spiritual wealth.

We finish with the Love of God chapter. It all starts and ends with God because God is love. In this chapter we explore the power of belief and what can happen when we give up control and let go of expectations.

HOW TO SUCCEED AT DOING WHAT YOU LOVE

Now let's unpack the second part of the subtitle. I want us all to succeed at doing what we love. This book serves as a guideline to help us do this. Keep in mind that you cannot define success for me and my life, so I won't attempt to define success for you and yours. Success is unique to the individual. We know, without anyone telling us, whether or not we feel and are successful. Although I won't try to define success for you, I will share how I've been able to do what I love, and earn an income doing it. I am thirty-four years old; I've never had a full-time job in my life. I make a living by writing, speaking and working with young people – all activities that I love to do.

One other thing. It's uncertain whether you or I know more about life and love. However, I know this isn't important. I believe that philosophers like Nas, Erykah Badu, Marianne Williamson, Deepak Chopra, Alice Walker, RZA, and Maya Angelou are as great as any Socrates or Plato. I know that circumstances and even truth is ever evolving. I know that most everything is subjective. Great minds, schools of thought and people come in many forms. I know that *great* is subjective too. Most importantly, what I *know* is what I believe and all that I believe comes from life experiences, observations and contact with a consciousness that none of us fully understands.

There are a few other things that I know for sure. I know that I am a work in progress and that I'm blessed beyond measure. I also know that I'm elated that you've decided to take this journey with me. Now let's get into it.

Introduction

Chapter 1
LOVE OF SELF

Message In The Music:

"I Will Make It"
by
KRS One

"Instead of reading the word of Christ,
BE the word of Christ
Instead of following God's word,
BE God's word
That's the consciousness of hip-hop
You are not just doing hip-hop, you ARE hip-hop
You are not just reading the word of God,
you ARE the word of God"

All of me
Yeah, that's right
Everything
That's my plight
Expose it all
Expose it now
Love
Of
Self
Three's a crowd
Just us two is all we need
Must go there
Cry
Maybe bleed
Heal a wound
Pick a scab
Loving Self isn't that bad
Despite the myths
Despite the news
Without love for me
I can't love you
Heal a scab
Pick a wound
Do what it is that works for you
Love of Self
Love of life
All of me
Yeah, that's right
Expose it all
It's not too late
The time is now
But at your pace
Do it for you and for me
For when you are you
I am free to be me
Love
of
Self

The first time that I witnessed racism hurt someone that I love, it happened in my living room one night after watching the 70s sitcom, *The Jeffersons*. George Jefferson, played by Sherman Hemsley, was the main character of the show – an unapologetically black, oftentimes rude but hilarious, businessman with a burgeoning dry cleaning company.

Although race was often a topic on the show and a springboard for stereotypically truthful humor to be catapulted from the minds of a more than likely white group of TV writers into homes across America, this particular episode dealt with race and race relations in an unusually serious way. On the episode, George saved a Ku Klux Klan member's life by performing CPR on him. Instead of thanking George, the man told George that he would rather have died than to have been saved by a Black man. Shortly after the show ended and the credits rolled away, my older brother Gil began to cry. He couldn't understand how the world could be so cruel to people who looked like us. My mom comforted my brother and explained to us yet again that this was our world's sad reality. She made it clear to my two brothers and me that we were different from the majority. We were Black and Puerto Rican boys and the world didn't expect much from us. We were going to be dead or in jail, period. This realization has always been a part of my identity, not by choice, but my default. I was taught from an early age that I had to love myself more than the world loved me. This is where my earliest sense of Love Of Self stemmed from.

Whether or not we are taught to love ourselves more because the world loves us less, from the time we are young too many of us are bombarded with expectations and boundaries, insults, and limitations that prohibit us from truly loving ourselves. So we must be bold and courageous about the way that we live our lives. What makes us happiest? How can we use our God-given talents to live out our dreams and contribute to society? I'm convinced that genuinely embracing a Love Of Self and following our unique God-given path may be part of the solution.

FOLLOW YOUR (GOD'S) PATH

Hanging on a wall in my room is a tattered and dingy *Creative Writing Award* that I received from Mrs. Gilbert in the second grade. I keep this award on my wall to remind myself that despite how bad society may try to make me feel about not owning a home or having great credit, if I follow God's plan I will always be wealthy.

In fourth grade Mrs. Preston sold me a typewriter. I remember it well. It was royal blue with black keys, and heavy for my boney arms to carry. I loved it though, and I loved the fact that Mrs. Preston saw a talent in me that prompted her to sell me her personal typewriter for only $1.00. In fifth grade Mrs. Becker encouraged me to enter a writing contest. I don't remember the topic of my essay or what happened to the savings bond that I won as a reward, but I do remember Mrs. Becker editing my essay the night before it was due so that I would make the deadline. I also remember my mom picking me up from school to go to the award ceremony at city hall. She was dressed in a champagne and navy blue skirt set and styled her hair in that mushroom cut that black women rocked in the 90s.

At home I had two parents and two brothers who believed in me. They willingly read my poetry and helped me develop my passion for writing by never being too busy or uninterested. I produced original poems and transcribed Maya Angelou's poetry into a composition style black and white notebook. Enthralled by the ingenious way that she would seamlessly sew words together, I wanted to do the same thing. I still have that composition notebook. Whenever I need motivation I look through the withered pages and remind myself of what my elementary thoughts once were.

The royal blue and black typewriter from Mrs. Preston wasn't the only typewriter I owned growing up. On my eighth birthday my parents gifted me the sequel, a more advanced gray typewriter. I'm sure I was the only kid in Oakbrook Projects who asked for a typewriter for his birthday. I could be wrong, but typewriters as birthday gifts for Black and Latino kids growing up in the projects wasn't the norm. Writing these pages has helped me to see how consistent God has been at telling me what to do with my life. It didn't matter that I lived in Oakbrook, a community where violence and drug abuse were routine parts of the day. God's plans couldn't be altered by those boundaries.

I loved everything about writing. From the way that it allowed me to express feelings to the way that my handwriting seemed to alter itself based on my mood alone. Once I got to high school I couldn't wait to write for the school newspaper. I covered topics like Jay-Z and Nas's rap battle, and the need for a curriculum that explored African American history beyond one elective class. I wrote for the newspaper all four years of high school and even represented the Journalism club on homecoming court. It wasn't really my thing but I was the only senior male in the club that year so I agreed to do it and came in third place.

But even with all of this writing and recognition throughout my childhood and young adult life, I still wasn't certain about my career goals. I knew I wanted to be a writer, but I didn't believe like Kanye believes in Kanye that it could actually happen. Somehow all of the signs that God had been giving me since the second grade weren't enough for me to accept my position and assignment as a writer.

Whether you've discovered what you're good at and love to do, or are still figuring it out, following your unique path will open you up to a world of opportunity. For example, I was recently approached about a business opportunity in the financial services field because of the work that I do as a writer. If all goes well, this business venture has the potential to be a lucrative investment for me that would've never been presented to me had I not been doing what I love as a writer and speaker.

*****

Not too long ago I wrote two newspaper articles about two people who are following their own unique paths. The first woman is a talented aerosol artist and friend of mine named Jaime. While interviewing Jaime I learned that as a child her older sibling would call her a "wicked witch." It was a way for Jaime's sibling to poke fun at her. Growing up, Jaime loved music and studied hip-hop dance. As an adult she worked as a manager at Staples while doing interior design work on the side. During this time, Jaime fell in love with graffiti and began to make friends within the art community in Philly. One day she tried her hand at making abstract aerosol paintings and discovered that she was pretty good at it. Next, she began helping a friend with commissioned pieces. After this she started making her own artwork. Finally, she found her niche creating portraits of the hip-hop superstars that she grew up listening to.

In the graffiti world it's common for artists to have a four letter nickname. This nickname needs to be short and sweet so it can be written quickly before anyone catches the person writing it. When it was time for Jaime to pick her graffiti handle she took the "wicked" from her childhood nickname and instead used the four letter spelling "WKiD." She also used this moniker as the name of her company, *WKiD Creations* (www.wkidcreations.com). The childhood nickname that she once disliked was now the perfect name for her business (and a dope one at that). This is the magic that happens when we follow our God-given paths. Had Jaime not been brave enough to do what she loves, her childhood nickname would mean nothing. Now, in some degree, it means everything. When you're on a path that aligns with the core of who you are and what you love to do, things have already been set in place for you to succeed on that path. Of course working hard, having faith, and conducting business with integrity will also help.

It's amazing when you sit back and look at the instances in your life that weave together one cohesive thread. Nothing that you've encountered or endured on your journey is by accident. There's a reason for every single thing you went through or are currently going through. Every bad time, missed opportunity, friendship, hobby, loss, and gain has a purpose in your life.

Here's another example. I recently had the pleasure of interviewing a woman named Mrs. Simmons. Mrs. Simmons is the owner of an antique furniture and vintage clothing store in Birdsboro, Pennsylvania. Throughout most of her adult life she worked in corporate accounting. For thirty of those years she collected antique furniture, clothing, and accessories and housed them in her basement. It was a pastime that her and her husband Gary loved. Their garage was filled with vintage leather coats, 90s era concert t-shirts, vinyl records, and a number of home goods inspired by decades past. When they had the time, they would set up at flea markets and sell their goods as a hobby. One day, after years of wrestling with the idea of owning her own shop, Mrs. Simmons decided that her desire for collecting vintage goods outweighed her desire to continue working for a large pest control company. So she put in her two-week notice, found an affordable store front, and hasn't looked back since.

Mrs. Simmon's first name is Grace. The name of Mrs. Simmons's store is *A Touch Of Grace*. Again, divine order made it so that everything was set in place waiting for Mrs. Simmons to claim what was already hers. The Universe already knew that when Mrs. Simmons decided to follow her heart and do what she loved, she would have the perfect name for her business. She worked hard, stepped out on faith and watched success unfold for her.

When I interviewed Mrs. Simmons she told me that what's most rewarding about owning *A Touch Of Grace* (213 E 1st St, Birdsboro, PA 19508) is that it allows her to bring joy to her customers by taking them down memory lane with her vintage wares. To some this may not seem like a big deal, but when you think about it, it's a blessing for Mrs. Simmons to bring this type of joy into people's lives. This is something that she was put on earth to do. *A Touch Of Grace* has been in business for three years and now includes bath and body products and a bi-annual fashion show.

When you make the decision to joyfully and willingly do what you love, whether as a hobby or career, you help contribute to the amount of happiness and joy that exists in the world. This is why we should only be doing what we absolutely love to do in order to earn a living. Making your passion your full-time job should always be the end goal, even if it takes five or ten years to make it happen. I began my journey to become a full-time writer six years ago and I'm just starting to get my size 9s wet as a professional writer. It takes time, diligence, hard work and dedication to turn something that you love into a full-time career.

*****

I didn't follow my own path. I followed the rules; whether unconsciously or consciously, I was influenced by my college advisor who didn't take my aspirations of being a writer seriously. I believed the society that told me that simply being in college was good enough. It always excites me to see young people following their dreams while they're still enrolled in high school or college. They're smarter than I was. For example, I met a college student in Philadelphia one weekend who wasn't old enough to have a glass of wine with me but was attending the same motivational coaching seminar that I was. It was hosted by speaker and philanthropist, Nehemiah Davis (Nehemiahdavis.com). It cost almost two hundred dollars, and took place on a Sunday evening. But there he was, the youngest person in the room, acquiring the knowledge needed to start a cleaning business so that he could be an employer instead of an employee. He was one of the most outgoing and vocal members of the group of mostly middle-aged adults.

I often wonder why society tries its best to make us believe that there's a good chance that our wildest dreams won't come true. While we're kids it's okay for us to have aspirations to be singers, writers, astronauts, actors, or even the president of the United States. But once we become teenagers that same society insists that we have a back-up plan just in case what we truly want doesn't happen.

There's a lot of problems with the public school system in the United States, but failing to teach our children to listen to and follow that inner voice that will guide them toward a life of fulfillment is one of its biggest problems. If you're a young person reading this, listen to that voice and use your God given talent now. There's no need to wait for a college degree or the right amount of courage, time, or money to get started. This goes for people my age and older as well. If you have a passion, start working on that passion today.

I've been a writer all of my life but it wasn't until I was twenty-eight years old that I finally had the courage to call myself one. Until then, the world had successfully convinced me that what God had planned was not good enough, that what was being shown to me since the second grade required a back-up plan. Crazy right? A back-up plan for God. God's love and intention needs no back-up plan.

*****

Oftentimes we believe the myth that we need to have everything figured out before we start with our creative and professional endeavors. That couldn't be further from the truth. We just have to be willing to jump in the pool, and then figure out how to swim once we're neck-deep in the water. You may not be able to do the back stroke on your first go round, but you'll soon see that your doggy paddle turns into laps around the pool. I do this all the time. When I began recording videos to promote this book and my lifestyle brand, Scared Of A Day Job, I didn't have a fancy camera or the money to purchase one so I began making videos on my android cell phone. They were blurry and didn't look anything like the videos I saw other influencers making. I didn't have a backdrop or a fancy introduction to my videos but I did my thing with what I had. I shot my videos guerilla style and spoke about topics that resonated with my audience. I did this for five months before I met a videographer. When it was time for us to start working together I was already comfortable talking to my followers and knew what I wanted my videos to look like. By starting on my own with the limited resources that I had, I was prepared for my blessing when it was time to level up.

"Wake up in the morning feelin' fresh to death
I'm so blessed"
– Jill Scott

START YOUR DAY THE RIGHT WAY

Developing a morning routine can be challenging. If you're stubborn like me, some days you'll decide that it's okay to lay in bed and scroll through Instagram first thing in the morning, so you do it (To my credit, I almost always use this time to expand my social media following by posting something relating to my work or interacting with my followers. If you're engaged in any type of entrepreneurial pursuit, this is important. But be better than me, don't do this first thing in the morning, no matter how tempting it might be). As helpful as social media is at connecting us to opportunities and like-minded people, it can also be a place where unnecessary chatter can have a field day with our minds. Sometimes I like to challenge myself by leaving my phone off until three or four in the afternoon (I made it until noon today). Whenever I do this I'm a lot more focused and productive. According to a study, 80 percent of people look at their phone within fifteen minutes of waking up in the morning. Try to be in the 20th percentile at least 90 percent of the time. Developing a morning routine will help with this.

Here's what I do: As soon as I open my eyes I say an internal "thank you" (sometimes I say it out loud too). I also put a big smile on my face. Next, I make my way to my sky blue yoga mat, which remains open on the far end of my living room. Once I'm on my mat I move through a few sun salutations, mountain poses, and cat cows to get my blood flowing. This puts me in tune with my body and aligns me with the earth's energy. After a handful of postures I feel present, grateful, and ready to do my best.

When I'm finished with yoga, I travel to the kitchen to fix myself a cup of warm lemon water. Drinking warm lemon water first thing in the morning rehydrates the body. It also flushes your digestive system so it can work at its full capacity throughout the day. I sip my lemon water while I write in my gratitude journal (we'll get into gratitude journals later). Next, I read a few pages out of a self-help or motivational book, or go directly into meditating. I try to meditate every morning (we'll get into the benefits of meditating later too). Most times I do, sometimes I don't. Although twenty minutes every day is the goal, there are days when my morning will only allow for ten minutes of stillness.

For most people, having any type of morning routine will require creativity. I understand that some of you don't have the luxury of working from home so you don't have as much time as I do in the morning. You may have a baby to tend to as soon as you open your eyes, or a meal to cook, or a bus to catch. Fine tuning your morning routine will take practice, and that's okay. Maybe you'll need to prepare your work clothes the night before so you can have more time in the morning. Or maybe you shower at night so that your mornings can be spent focusing inward. Like everything in life, we prioritize that which is important to us, a morning routine is no different. You have to decide that having a morning routine is important to your well-being and success. Once you make this decision, you'll figure out a way to get it done. Your day will run a lot smoother because of it too. Not to mention, having a morning routine is one of the many ways we practice Love Of Self.

Some of you may think creating a morning routine is impossible. But starting somewhere is better than not starting at all. It could be that before you begin your busy day you lay in bed an extra three minutes and think about one or two things that you have to be thankful about (the breakfast you're going to eat, the eyes that you just opened, the apartment that you're in – the list could literally go on and on). And when you're ready, maybe you'll take it a step further and write these things down. Before you know it you will have created an individualized and doable morning routine.

*****

Two days ago I met a man named Andrè Young. Andrè is the CEO of life enrichment company, *You Evolving Now* (www.youevolvingnow.com). When Andrè and I were introduced to one another by a man named Ion (I'll tell you more about Ion later), we hit it off quickly. During our conversation, Andrè said something to me that made a lasting impression. He told me that he couldn't remember the last time that he had a bad morning. Andrè likes to do something that he calls "bookending" his day. Every morning he sends encouraging text messages to the members of *You Evolving Now*. These members also have access to Andrè's website, which he updates daily with inspirational blog posts and videos.

Preparing these blog posts and text messages at night, and then sending them out first thing in the morning, "bookends" Andrè's day with positivity. He spends his nights preparing these inspiring messages and goes to sleep with them on his mind. When he wakes in the morning the first thing that he does is send out the text messages while he works on his motivational blog post for the day. Andrè loves what he does and figured out a way to guarantee that his mornings are as positive as possible. I understand that some of you reading may not love what you do yet. When we're working at jobs that we don't love it's not easy to wake up in the morning excited about the day ahead of us. If you know that you're about to go to a job that you despise, you have to do everything in your power to make sure that your day is as productive and positive as possible. You also have to believe that you have the ability to create something better for yourself, and that something better is on its way.

To help you get started creating a morning routine, I've provided space for you to outline what you want your routine to look like. If you already have a morning routine, use the space to fine tune what you're already doing.

My morning routine includes/will include:

_____

_____

_____

FINDING & ACKNOWLEDGING YOUR GIFT

Nothing is by chance. Curiosity is God given. It's not a coincidence that you enjoy decorating your house, or attending a fashion show, or teaching a child how to solve a math problem. These types of activities correlate with your personal and unique talents and abilities. It's your responsibility to use them to improve your life and the lives of those around you. Your interests, dislikes, comforts, and discomforts are all a part of a grand design. Embrace this and view these character traits as opportunities with limitless potential.

Once you recognize that thing that you can't go a day without thinking about, you've discovered your gift. The next thing you have to do is figure out how you're going to re-gift it to the world. I got lucky. My talent and passion were shown to me at a young age, which then led to me discovering other talents and passions. For example, my passion for working with young people was revealed to me in my junior year of college at West Chester University. I discovered it by way of my first true love. Because I did well in Dr. Hannah Ashley's writing class, she offered me a position as a writing tutor for a program called *Writing Zones 2.0*. In this position I helped high school students become better writers and realized that I had a natural ability to work with young people. Before this, all I knew about tutoring was that I needed it in order to pass the most basic of math classes in my freshman year of college. Had I not been willing to step out of my comfort zone I most likely would have never unearthed my affinity for educating young people. Once I graduated college my tutoring position with *Writing Zones* helped me to land my first professional job as a college adviser at my alma mater, Reading Senior High School.

We've all been blessed with talent. If you haven't discovered yours yet, you may just have to dig a little deeper and take inventory of your life. Start to take note of which of your hobbies and interests stand out to you the most. What makes you come alive and feel the most joy? Remember what it was like to wake up on a bitter cold December morning to find out that school was cancelled because of a snowstorm? I'm talking about that type of joy. Once you figure this out you'll begin connecting the dots of synchronicity that will help map out which path you should follow.

*****

Sometimes born leaders aren't aware of their inherent talent to lead and to stand firmly in leadership positions. This reminds me of a friend of mine named Carissa. As long as I've known Carissa she's been a go-getter. In our senior year of high school she ran for class president. She managed a smart campaign, and even wore pink extensions in her hair so that she would stand out amongst the other candidates. It was close, but she unfortunately lost the race. Once we graduated high school Carissa studied Criminal Justice at Widener University. During that time we stayed in touch minimally and became reacquainted more recently through the work that we do in my hometown, Reading, Pennsylvania.

After graduating college, Carissa started her career in the social justice field working as a case worker at Berks County Jail System. She was also a weekend counselor during this time, conducting individual counseling for victims of domestic and sexual violence. She stayed busy – two jobs and a personal life, but she still found time to volunteer with a number of non-profit and grassroots organizations in our city. Most recently, she became a Magisterial District Judge, the first African American female in Berks County to hold this seat.

One day while having lunch with Carissa she revealed to me that she didn't know what her talent was. I didn't understand. I asked her to clarify and told her how surprised I was that she wasn't aware of her many talents. Being a community leader and having a genuine desire to help people are two of Carissa's many gifts. I reminded her that she has been putting herself in positions of leadership since we were teenagers skipping school to go to King of Prussia Mall. I reassured her that co-founding organizations, running a political campaign, and being a change agent in an impoverished city takes a tremendous amount of talent. She listened but didn't say much. The next day Carissa wrote a Facebook post about our conversation and publicly thanked me for helping her acknowledge a few of her many talents.

Sometimes our society – with its infatuation with material possessions, celebrities, and sports – gets lost in the sauce of what talent is and isn't. Talent comes in many forms. It's individual. My talents were picked precisely for me, and yours were chosen intentionally for you.

Think about the activities that you love to do. Now think about your dream job. What came to mind? What you love to do and your dream job should be directly related to one another. This isn't by coincidence. That which you love to do has a purpose in your life. It's up to you to decide whether you will treat these activities as mere hobbies or give them the respect that they deserve.

My dream job is to serve as a:

_____

Defining and then writing your dream job down and believing that you can have it is the first step toward attracting it into your life. Next, you need to say it out loud. Calling yourself exactly what God has created you to be is necessary. It's empowering too. If you're an artist call yourself one. Words have power. In my view, God isn't an entity that needs to be worshipped, but if that's an ideology that you subscribe to, I challenge you to consider calling yourself what God has created you to be as one of the highest forms of worship.

Notice the phrasing in the statement that I used. Instead of using the word *work*, I purposely used the word *serve*. To do what you love to do is to serve. In *One Day My Soul Just Opened Up* by Iyanla Vanzant, Vanzant writes about the act of honoring ourselves and others with service. She writes: "Service is the act of doing what you love for the sake of loving it. This is the highest work you can do in the world. Service is the divine multiplier. When you perform an act of genuine service, giving of your time, energy, and resources as an act of love, the universe will multiply what you do and reward you with greater results than expected." I couldn't agree with this statement more. Think of the work that you do as a service. How can you use your gifts to serve others? There's a unique joy that sweeps over us when we re-gift our gifts in the form of service.

DON'T STRAY TOO FAR OFF OF THE PATH

I took my first styling job in elementary school. I remember it clearly. My friend Dennis and I were jumping around on his twin bed when somehow the topic of what he would wear for school pictures came up. Since he wasn't sure yet, I leaped into action. I picked out beige khakis, a white t-shirt, and an earth tone sweater vest. Fresh. I think I still have that discolored class picture somewhere. As an adult I've worked very minimally as a stylist, both for pay and not for pay. Oftentimes, I'm the go-to person in the family when wedding attire needs to be picked out or when my mom isn't sure which shoes will match best with her church outfit. I've also written for a few fashion websites.

Despite having this interest in fashion, being a stylist and working in the fashion industry isn't what I should be doing right now. I realized this after spending time, money, and energy attempting to start a business selling men's thrift clothing. Then one day it hit me – I haven't mastered how to sell books or my speaking services! Why am I trying to sell clothes? It's funny when I think about it now. I'm not sure what I was thinking, but I do know that there's value in trying and failing. So keep trying, keep failing, and keep learning!

Reselling thrift store clothing is a bit of a stretch for me and my path at the moment. Because my life's purpose is to write and help as many people as possible, it makes more sense for me to focus my energy on writing and speaking, not clothing sales. I'm all about having multiple hustles, though they just need to work together. For example, selling my own brand of clothing that shares the same name of my lifestyle brand and writing and speaking company makes a lot more sense.

I had already begun thinking that selling thrift clothing had the potential to take me away from my life's mission, but there was one situation that took place on a hot summer day that solidified it for me. As I walked from the gas station to my apartment in search of a funnel, I was regretting my decision to wear sweatpants. The car that I was driving ran out of fuel and I wasn't happy about it. Salty beads of sweat were making their way down my face as I took long strides over one of the world famous Reading railroad tracks. Then I heard the blare of a car horn and saw a familiar face. It was Jonathan, a personable and ambitious guy in his early 20s. I was introduced to Jonathan a few months prior when I interviewed him and wrote a story about his clothing company Visonare (www.vsnre.com). Luckily, he pulled over to see if I needed a ride and offered to let me use his funnel. I took him up on his offer and hopped in his vanilla-colored Chrysler. As we headed back to where I was parked we got reacquainted and filled one another in on our entrepreneurial endeavors.

A few days before this Jonathan and I spoke about me hiring him to take photos of me for my website and thrift clothing sales. Although Jonathan is not a photographer, photography had become a way for him to supplement his income while building his clothing brand empire. When I inquired about setting up a photoshoot with him Jonathan's reply made it crystal clear as to why he was there to offer me a ride. I quickly realized that it could've been anyone. Reading is a small city and I know a lot of people, but the Universe sent him for a reason.

Jonathan told me that he was no longer doing photography because he needed to focus solely on establishing Visonare as a sought after clothing brand. Lightbulb moment. This idea of only focusing on one endeavor at a time wasn't anything that I hadn't heard before, but it was the confirmation that I needed to hear at that moment. I understood what I needed to do. This is how the Universe works when you follow your path and remain open to receiving help from an entity bigger than yourself. The Universe will always provide situations and people that we can learn from, but we have to be willing to listen. Then we must apply the lessons once we've learned them. The next day I deleted all of the thrift clothing related photos on my Instagram account and began using the social media platform to advertise myself strictly as a writer and speaker.

There will be time for me to delve further into the world of fashion, but right now is not that time. Part of following your path and creating a successful life for yourself is having the ability to discern the right time to use each of your gifts. Prayer and meditation can help with this. Having mentors who can guide you along the way is also helpful.

What's one ability or talent that might be holding you back from your true calling and purpose?

_____

_____

Is it possible for you to cultivate this talent without it taking you away from what you are meant to be doing at this particular time in your life? How can you do this?

_____

_____

_____

<u>The 4 Agreements by Don Miguel Ruiz</u>:

1. Be impeccable with your word.

2. Do not take anything personally.

3. Do not make any assumptions

4. ALWAYS DO YOUR BEST

When you have a Love Of Self doing your best comes naturally. It's not always the easiest thing to do, but it becomes a way of life that takes practice. Fortunately, we always reap the greatest rewards for our work when we decide to work at our passions joyfully, with the intent of doing our best for ourselves and those around us. When we combine doing our best with being relentless we're unstoppable. It took me almost two years and several e-mails to get a freelance writing job at the newspaper in my city. When the Lifestyle editor didn't respond to my emails I would wait a few weeks and email her back, politely asking if any new writing opportunities had arose. Finally, she gave me a shot. Once I got the green light it was on me to take the ball and run with it. I did my very best on that first article and have been writing for the newspaper ever since.

*****

If I had it my way, I would the travel the world nonstop and craft the pages of my books and articles while sitting on a beach that also serves as my backyard. My mind would be at ease and my skin lathered in coconut oil while being admired by the sun's rays. But I'm not there yet. Until I'm able to make this dream a reality, I have to do my best with everything else that I'm doing. It's a practice that has paid off for me numerous times. I even attended graduate school for free as a result of me doing my best. Here's how it happened.

After earning my bachelor's degree from West Chester University I began working as a college adviser for the Talent Search program at Reading Senior High School. After my first year of working for Talent Search we were approached by Kutztown University about a partnership that would allow us to expose our students to life on a college campus. The partnership would culminate in a new program called, *The Granted Access Project*. Due to my success as a college adviser, I was chosen to be the coordinator of *The Granted Access Project*. This new role allowed me to expand my network and earn more money. It also gave me the opportunity to build a relationship with my new boss Rhonda, the director of the Multicultural Center.

While in this position, I became curious about obtaining my Master's Degree. I became even more interested when I learned that I could attend graduate school without having to pay for it. All I had to do was work twenty hours per week as a graduate assistant at the Multicultural Center. Because I already had a relationship with Rhonda, and had been doing my best as the coordinator of *The Granted Access Project*, it was fairly easy for me to get that assistantship position. This then led to more opportunity.

Part of my job as a graduate assistant at the Multicultural Center was to coordinate monthly leadership workshops for male students on campus. I either led the workshop or hired a speaker to facilitate the workshop for me. I learned two things because of this new responsibility. I learned that I had a natural ability to create and present engaging and informative workshops, and I also learned that workshop facilitators make good money to speak for one hour. I quickly realized that I could do what these speakers were doing and be just as good as they were, if not better. Once I finished my assistantship, I started my speaking career.

Doing my best in my position as an educator while I make the transition to a full-time writer and speaker has been crucial to my journey. Admittedly, it's not difficult for me to do my best because I actually like my job as an educator. I understand that this isn't the case for many people reading this book. I am fully aware that some of you may have dreams of being a clothing designer or an airplane pilot, while working as a lunch aide at an elementary school, or a sales associate at a shoe store. If you fall into this category, it's even more important for you to do your best at your current position, whatever it is. When we're doing our best opportune moments will inevitably find us. But we have to believe that they will and put in the work to make it happen!

It's one thing to be forced to go to a job that you hate, but it's another thing to make that experience worse by dreading every minute of it once you're there. Whatever you're doing, own it. If you're the sales clerk at a supermarket with aspirations of becoming a big time record producer, be the best sales clerk in the store. Be someone your boss can count on and embrace the fact that opportunity sometimes disguises itself as sacrifice and hard work (also try to get a job in the music industry, even if it's as a janitor in a recording studio or working as an unpaid intern at a record label). Once you build that healthy relationship with the boss she might let you play music from a small radio while you check-out customers. Guess whose music and beats you can play on that radio, your own. Rappers, singers, record label executives, and A&R's need groceries too. The aspiring record producer, grocery store clerk has to believe that anything is possible.

It's important to remain in a state of believing that something good is always on its way – that we deserve to live abundant lives – that it's possible to go from janitor to airplane pilot, from grocery store clerk to Grammy award winning record producer. In my case, from a kid raised in one of the poorest cities in the country, to a *New York Times* Best-Selling author.

PATIENCE & DISCIPLINE

A reminder to "Be Patient & Disciplined" is written on a post-it note that hangs on the wall above my desk at my home office. I keep this post-it note there to remind me that patience and discipline must work together – like Martin and Gina, like Will & Grace. One without the other won't work. If I'm too patient I'll wait for circumstances outside of my control to dictate my next move. I won't reach out to colleges about speaking engagements, or inquire with magazines about freelance work. If I'm all discipline and no patience, I'll get discouraged with how long it's taking me to accomplish my goals. There has to be a balance so that both patience and discipline can collaborate.

If you're an entrepreneur, having patience and discipline is crucial. It'll help you to take breaks and carve out time for family and fun when you need to so that you don't burn out. Part of having a Love Of Self is giving yourself the permission to take breaks as often as you need to.

Not matter how long it takes for you to be able to call the activities that you love your full-time job, the journey will be worth it, because it's your journey that adds value to your story. If you're a business owner your story is essential to your brand. An interesting story is one of the best marketing tools that you can have no matter what type of business you own. People want to know your story, they want to relate to it, be inspired by it, and use it as fuel for their own journey.

"God does not want us to believe in the concept of God beyond more than we believe in the concept of the God within. As much as we look up to God in faith, we must also look within and believe that we have the answers or have been blessed with the means to seek them out. For this reason, minus ego, we must believe in ourselves just as much as we believe in God. This is Love Of Self."

SAVE YOURSELF

Most of us have been taught to look for a savior externally, but the answers are almost always within. More often than not our authentic self is the savior that we need. When people hit rock bottom they begin searching for someone or something to save them. Ironically, the thing, entity or person that they are looking for is themselves. They're in search of who they were before the world got a hold of them – before class and capitalism, prejudice, bias, self-doubt, and judgment became a part of their psyche.

We were not born into sin or to be saved by Jesus Christ, or anyone else. If you believe that Jesus was and is a savior, I challenge you to also believe that you are a savior. Because like Jesus, we were all born to be saviors – saviors for our families, saviors for our communities, and saviors for this world. Luckily, there are people like you who are beginning to shift the paradigm – people who know that they can save themselves. The reason that you can save yourself is because you were made in the image of God. In India it is not uncommon for people to consider themselves Gods. The term for this is Pantheism. It is a belief that everything and everyone is God, and God is everything and everyone. However, this doesn't mean that we don't need God's help and guidance. In fact, it means the opposite. Having a Love Of Self is realizing that it is only with God's help and infinite wisdom, that we have the ability to take control of our lives. When we realize this our world will begin to develop in new and exciting ways.

EMBRACE YOUR WHOLE SELF

In Alice Walker's *Anything We Love Can Be Saved*, Walker writes about religion's role in teaching us not to embrace our "shadow." She writes: "When you're taught God loves you, but only if you're good, obedient, trusting and so forth, and you know you're that way only some of the time, there's a tendency to deny your shadow side." Part of having a Love Of Self is learning to embrace and celebrate our thoughts, imagination, ideas, and feelings, as well as our flaws and our shortcomings. Oftentimes, these flaws represent a side of our being, with its inherent dualistic nature, that needs more of our attention and love, not because it's our better or worse side but because we haven't been taught to embrace it and use it to our advantage. We are better off when we acknowledge all of ourselves. When we consciously work on these shortcomings and flaws instead of letting them control us, or just as bad, deem ourselves unworthy of God's love because of them, they become easier to navigate.

In *The Shadow Effect*, authors Deepak Chopra, Debbie Ford, and Marianne Williamson explore how embracing this "shadow side" can be beneficial to us. The authors believe that in order to reach our full potential, we must welcome both the positive and negative charges of our nature. For example, if someone acknowledges that they struggle with lust they can use tools like meditation, mindfulness, and yoga to keep lust in its proper place. It's important to remember that it's the "struggle" that categorizes lust as an aspect of their personality that they may need to pay closer attention to, not the societal influenced assumption that lust is "bad" or belongs to a "shadow" side. If this person suppresses this aspect of their personality without acknowledging that it exists, it will be more difficult for them to control it. In order to manage anything we have to first recognize that it exists. When we do this we put ourselves in a position to control it instead of letting it control us. If someone is in a committed relationship and they know that lust is an issue for them, the first thing that they need to do is acknowledge that it's an issue. Next, they need to communicate it with their partner. Once their partner is aware of this, lust is no longer something that they need to suppress and hide. This could then open the door to all types of fun for them and their partner.

Debbie Ford writes: "The reason for doing shadow work is to become whole, to end our suffering, to stop hiding from ourselves. Once we do this, we can stop hiding from the rest of the world." Part of doing this shadow work that Ford writes about involves accepting that we're not perfect so we won't always have perfect thoughts, intentions and feelings, and that's okay.

She goes on to say: "We have to uncover, own, and embrace all of who we are, the good and bad, the light and the dark, the selfless and the selfish, and the honest and dishonest parts of our personality. It is our birthright to be whole, to have it all. But to do this, we must be willing to take an honest look at ourselves and step out beyond our judgmental mind. It is here that we will have a life-altering shift in perception, an opening of our heart." While I do agree that we all have aspects of our personality that are great as well as aspects of our personality that are not so great, it's important to be cognizant of the language that we use to describe these different parts of our personality. Ford mentions that we must be willing to "step out of our judgmental mind" so that we can have a shift in perception and an opening of our heart. I agree with her to an extent. However, I'm not convinced that it's possible to step out of our "judgmental mind" if we are splitting ourselves up into two sides and labeling one "light" and the other "dark." By using this language we invite judgment in instead of stepping away from it. We know inherently that darkness represents negativity while light represents positivity. We also know that we can't have light without darkness. I'd like to think that embracing our whole self without labeling one side as dark or light is a kinder, gentler, and more loving way to accept the many sides of our complex personalities. When we do this it will be reflected in all areas of our lives – from our relationships to our careers to the way that we embrace our communities.

Chapter 2
LOVE OF COMMUNITY

Message In The Music:

"One"
by
Mary J. Blige & U2

"One love, one blood
One life, you got to do what you should
One life with each other
Sisters, brothers
One life, but we're not the same
We get to carry each other, carry each other
One
One"

Commune
Be with me as I am with you
Hold my hand
Help me see this through
Be my guide
Let me give you guidance too
Speak my language
And I'll try to speak yours too
Commune

The plain clothes undercover cop waved his gun in our direction as he ran up Liggett Avenue in the Oakbrook Projects on a sunny Saturday afternoon. He was on one end of the block and the man that he was prepared to exchange fire with was on the other end. My brother and I were in the crossfire. One of the men, I can't remember which, wore a gray and blue color blocked sweatshirt and stone washed blue jeans, his black gun complimenting the colors of his outfit. Before I knew it a jolt of fear and urgency swept over me as I caught a glimpse of my dad's face as he ran up the block. Like most of my neighbors, he was watching the drug bust that went sour and resulted in a foot chase and a possible shootout.

My dad couldn't get to my brother and me in time and he knew it. Frantically, he gestured for us to go into my friend Dennis's apartment as he ran toward our home on the opposite end of the block. A bike was thrown into Dennis's backroom and my brother and I weren't far behind it. Now in the living room, we were shook up but we were safe. This was Oakbrook projects on a bad day. *On the good days, and there were plenty of them, Oakbrook was a place where there was a thriving sense of community. This is where I spent the first ten years of my life.*

COMMUNAL ACTIVITIES IN OAKBROOK

Not all of the communal activities that took place in Oakbrook were legal but they were ours. We owned them and we were proud to be from OB. When the grownups needed beer they didn't drive into town or take the bus there, they knocked on Mrs. Montana's door and bought a single or six pack of Budweiser. If you needed weed you knocked on my door. For years I never realized that my dad sold weed and that he and my mom smoked it. I was the youngest, the most oblivious. When my brother and I would find the silver tray, hidden under our chocolate brown couch, we would marvel at the clear plastic bag filled to the brim with weed. We would smell the green substance that looked like oregano, but never dared to touch it.

Oakbrook is the place where I learned how to fight, respect my elders, and stand up for myself. It was a place where it didn't take much to keep my brothers and me happy and occupied. On summer nights we stayed out late under the care of everyone on our block as we played every type of tag known to man. When we were indoors my family of five was tight knit, even though we had our problems like most communities do. I can remember my mother and father fighting like they hated one another, but those aren't the memories that have resonated with me after all these years. What I remember most is community and love. I remember breakfast in bed when it was someone's birthday. I remember my brothers being my first best friends.

Although my oldest brother Nick was a few years older than Gil and me, he always made time for us. As far as I could tell he didn't mind, and my parents wouldn't have it any other way even if he did. I remember my dad wearing a blue and yellow headband and short shorts while he flipped burgers on the grill or pushed us around on the basketball court in an attempt to make us tough. I remember the smell of Pine sol in the morning as Smokey Robinson's "Tears of a Clown" or "Cruisin'" blasted out of the gray stereo system. When we heard Smokey and smelled Pine Sol on a Saturday morning we knew it was time to clean. How else would all of that brass get dusted? My mom loved brass. We had one of the cleanest cribs in the projects too. On inspection day the animated woman from the housing authority would leave just as soon as she came because our home was always spotless, especially on inspection day.

Our small three bedroom row home style apartment wasn't a party house, but there were plenty of parties that took place there. Birthday parties, cookouts, fight parties that ended quickly because Mike Tyson would knock his opponent out in the first round, New Years Eve parties and WWF wrestling parties. This is how we communed with each other and our community.

WHAT IS LOVE OF COMMUNITY?

The word community is derived from the Latin word *communis*, which means "common." So when we think of the word *community*, we must consider the commonalities and traits that bind us together as humans sharing a common space. When we have a love of community we realize that whether we want to admit it or not, we are all in this thing together. Having a Love Of Community means that we see value in being in this together and put others before self. This is Love Of Community.

Deliberately caring for the planet is how we express Love Of Community on a macro level. It might mean that we adopt a plant based diet because we know that eating meat harms animals and the environment. On a micro scale, community is really everything. Our families are our communities. The places we work and frequent are a part of our community.

Fully embracing a Love Of Community allows us to look at every person that we encounter as a reflection of God's love. This means that despite religious background, sexual orientation, class, or ethnicity, we are able to see the God inside of every person we encounter. Obviously, this is easier said than done. We don't always want to see the God inside someone who treats us bad, cuts us off in traffic, or talks about us behind our back. But the truth is, the people who do these kinds of things need the most love. Trying our best to give this love away to everyone who we encounter is how we embrace Love Of Community on a micro level.

Having a Love Of Community doesn't make you an extrovert who loves being around people all the time either. We all have those days when we're out in public praying that we don't run into someone that we know. This doesn't mean that we don't have a Love Of Community, it just means that I'd like to buy my organic waffles and peanut butter without having to engage in small talk with Maria from my 9th grade algebra class. Keep in mind, Maria may need your help in some way, or may be able to help you – so more often than not, speak to her anyway, even if you look like shit and don't feel like talking – you never know what might come of that conversation.

*****

Here's an example of what can happen when fear trumps Love Of Community. After moving out of Oakbrook Projects at the age of ten my family and I relocated to a lower-middle class neighborhood in a suburb called Millmont. We were the only minority family on our block at the time, and we were treated as such. On more than one occasion Gil and I had to fight neighborhood kids because we represented difference. We didn't want to fight, but we weren't going to let them disrespect us or call us niggers either.

As the years went by the neighborhood became more diverse, and our family became a bit more accepted and acclimated to the new surroundings. After about ten years of living in Millmont, to everyone's surprise, a mosque opened up directly behind our home. Every Friday our quiet, predominantly white, neighborhood came alive with Muslim people of all shades. They took up all of the parking and occasionally parked on private property. Other than this, they minded their business and just wanted to congregate in peace, the same way that members of the Christian church just two blocks away congregated in peace every Sunday.

My neighbors would yell the most ignorant things you could imagine at the Muslim people attending the mosque. "Go back to where you come from" they yelled as if my high school friend Muhammad who attended the mosque with his family wasn't born in the United States. Difference proved to be an unfortunate barrier. Instead of enriching a neighborhood, it did the opposite. Instead of initiating intrigue and healthy curiosity, difference served as a catalyst for fear. I think about what education could have done. What if my neighbors knew that Christianity and Islam share more commonalities than differences, that both groups worship the same God but call that God different names? Allah is Arabic for God. They didn't think about the fact that a Muslim praying to Allah is the same thing as a Christian praying to God. I'm sure most of them never realized that a man who speaks Arabic is not referring to God as Allah because he has a different God than a Christian has. This is why education is so important. Education has the potential to birth spiritual and religious tolerance. Tolerance is everything. It is the foundation on which common ground and acceptance can begin to be built upon.

RELIGIOUS TOLERANCE IN ACTION

A sense of uneasiness came over me as I prepared to remove myself from the prayer circle formed by my aunts, uncles, and cousins at Thanksgiving dinner. My abuela was there too, quietly observing everything, like she always does. This was the first time that I wouldn't be praying with my family. "It's okay, he doesn't have to pray," my uncle said nonchalantly as I let two hands coming from opposite directions enclose in front of me and officially take me out of the circle. "He's going to pray," my aunt mumbled quietly, "just in his own way." As I sat there and watched my family talk to Jesus I felt a little awkward to not be included in the conversation. I was proud of myself though and I knew that if Jesus had been there he would've been proud too.

In this moment my family is able to see past their personal views and respect my decision to pray to the energy that is God as opposed to the Jesus that is man. Do they agree with my decision? Of course not. But they respectfully tolerate it nonetheless. With this equal exchange of understanding both my family and I are taking this experience and using it to create a more loving and tolerant environment in spite of our different takes on prayer and religion. They do their part by continuing to welcome me in their home and not making an issue out of me not praying with the family, and I do my part by standing in my truth. And probably without realizing it, we set an example for the younger generation who is watching from the sidelines.

RELIGIOUS INTOLERANCE IN ACTION

One fall afternoon while at the same uncle's house, without invitation or warning, a friend of the family began talking to me about God and Christianity with the clear intention of "saving me." I wasn't interested in a religious debate, so I didn't say much. The verbal exchange was still offensive though. I was told that my eyes were closed to God's truth because I was a "non-believer." The day before this conversation I completed a five day fast. It was a time of reflection, limited eating, prayer, meditation, and yoga. Needless to say, I was feeling extremely close to God and very much open to God's truth.

During that same visit the same friend of the family told those of us in the family who weren't Christians that we were forfeiting our right to see my deceased grandfather in the afterlife. By this point in my life being insulted because of my relationship with God was nothing new to me, but this one took the cake. I remember looking around the room in an attempt to capture the expressions on the faces of those of us who were not Christians. The audacity I thought, as I struggled to understand how someone could say something so hurtful to us. As my eyes fixed their gaze toward two of my aunts I felt a pit in my stomach for them. One of them left the room. Whether or not I believe in the "afterlife" or not doesn't take away from the fact that my aunts had been told that they wouldn't see their dad again because of they way they choose to love God.

Conversations like these exist as the unfortunate norm when religion is used as a divider instead of a unifier. Someone's personal relationship with God is just that, personal. It's not something that should be discussed or questioned unless both parties welcome the discussion and questioning. While the intention of the conversations at my uncle's house that day may have been aimed at the highest good, the result and outcome of those conversations brought about exclusivity, rejection, and feelings of discontent.

When we look at someone through a personal lens that has been influenced by a system like religion, it becomes difficult for us to see the God in that person if they belong to a group that is outside of the group that we belong to. But here's the thing, we don't have time for anything that doesn't unite us and bring us together. Now more than ever we must be unified so that we can figure out ways to augment society's most dangerous and unequal ills. In short, we have to always choose love.

ALWAYS CHOOSE LOVE

Not too long ago I made a decision that required me to choose love and Love Of Community over my personal feelings. While attending my cousin's wedding my Tio Anibal suggested that I write a newspaper article about a group of Christian men who call themselves *The Knights*. To be honest, I wasn't thrilled about the idea of writing an article about *The Knights*. But I wasn't opposed to learning more about the group to see if a potential story was there. I agreed to attend a *Knights* meeting the following Thursday and invited my Dad to go along with me.

When we arrived at the small room in the mansion-like popular church we found close to a dozen mostly middle-aged men of different ethnicities sitting around a table talking about personal topics generated from a video clip that they had just watched. The men spoke freely and shared testimonies that they probably wouldn't have shared with other men in a different setting. It was a safe space. I didn't participate in the open discussion, but I found it to be engaging and insightful, even if I didn't agree with everything that was being said.

Once we left, I told my dad that, although I didn't have a bad time and was happy to have attended, I wasn't sure if I was going to pitch the story to my editor. I was hesitant to write an article that would potentially promote Christianity. I thought about my personal beliefs and what my local following might think of me writing a book about making love my religion, while also being paid to write a story about a Christian men's group. I told my dad that I would meditate on it and get back to him and my uncle about my decision.

That night as I sat on my couch in my basement apartment listening to a vinyl recording of Stevie Wonder's "Have A Talk With God" from his *Songs In The Key Of Life* album, I decided that I would write the story. I didn't need to meditate in the traditional sense to make my decision. My decision was made when I thought about *The Knights* and how they interacted with and supported one another. I knew that other men in my city needed to feel the love that I felt while I was at the meeting.

While it's never my intent to promote organized religion, I have to always choose love and Love Of Community over my personal feelings. Every time. There was love in that room, I couldn't deny that. I decided that it was my responsibility to help other men feel that love, even at the expense of my own beliefs.

YOU CAN'T DO IT ALONE: HELP OTHERS & LET THEM HELP YOU

What if every time we accomplished something we celebrated that accomplishment by helping someone? Think about how rewarding that would be for everyone involved. Love Of Community is about recognizing that you can't do everything on your own, and whether your endeavors be artistic, entrepreneurial, or otherwise, you need to accept help from others and you need to help other people. As you accomplish new goals you have to help those around you accomplish new goals too. Maybe it's not an individual person or group of people that you help, maybe it's a non-profit organization, a soup kitchen or a library in your neighborhood. A few hours of volunteering or a small donation can go a long way.

What three people/organizations can you help without expecting anything in return?

1. _____

2. _____

3. _____

Helping others produces helpful energy in your own life. You extend a hand, a hand gets extended to you, and this energy is recycled over and over again. This is how the Universe works. But we can't give expecting to get. To expect something in return poisons the spirit of giving at its root. Never expect anything in return. Knowing that good fortune will come back to you is different than *expecting* good fortune to come back to you. When you expect, you wait. When you know, you treat that good fortune as if it has already come back because you know that it will.

*****

So many times when people are looking to get mentored by someone they immediately ask that person for help instead of first asking the person how they might be able to help them. People like helping people who are helpful. The next time you reach out to someone for help consider offering help before asking for anything. For example, there's someone in a similar field as me who I would like to work with and be mentored by. Instead of asking this person for help or even to be my mentor, I first established a relationship with them by offering my help. This is what I did. I noticed that when they posted pictures to their Instagram account they weren't using hashtags to drive traffic to their posts. So I sent them an email explaining the importance of hashtags and provided a list of popular ones they could use. The whole thing including the "research" and the email took no more than ten minutes. This person appreciated my gesture and employed the strategies that I suggested. Although they haven't seen a huge spike in the amount of followers that they have, there appears to have been some gains made. Now when I need help this person might be more willing to help me because they recognize that I've sincerely tried to help them without expecting anything in return.

CONNECT

Have you ever noticed that successful, happy people have mastered the art of connection? Some people are born with this skill, and others, like me, have to sharpen it. Figure out where you land on the connector scale, then adjust accordingly. If you're someone who isn't a "born connector," practice until you get better at it. You can start by attending networking events and challenging yourself to authentically connect with three people. After this, try five people, then seven, then ten, until you've mastered the art of connection. Another way to practice connecting with people is to start conversations with strangers. It doesn't have to be weird or awkward either. If you're in your favorite café and you see someone that you don't recognize, introduce yourself and start a conversation with that person. I met my website designer this way. He was sitting quietly in Mi Casa Su Casa on Penn Street (my second office) when I noticed that he was someone whom I'd never seen there before. So I introduced myself and started a conversation. From that conversation I learned that he was an educator, website designer, and videographer. After talking for few minutes I shared with him that I wasn't happy with my website, so he offered to help me revamp it at no cost. Had I not made that connection I might have never put myself in a position to save hundreds of dollars and connect with a local educator and like-minded individual.

Not too long ago I met a man in the financial services field named Ion. Ion is a born connector. He's full of energy and happy to learn from everyone that he meets. In addition to the fact that it benefits his business to interact with as many people as possible, it's clear that Ion loves connecting. It's also clear that people genuinely love connecting with him. I know this because whenever I meet someone who knows Ion they always have something to say about how helpful he is or how fruitful their relationship with him is. He's the ultimate connector. I've only known Ion for eight months, but through our working relationship I've grown my professional network, gained five freelance writing assignments, and learned about two networking groups, one of which I now belong to. Long story short, meet Ions; be an Ion.

TRANSFORMATIONAL MOMENT: LOVE OF COMMUNITY IN ACTION

One of my first articles for the *Reading Eagle* newspaper involved writing a story about a community activist, dancer, and artist named Daniel. Daniel's a native of Peru with a passion for the arts and community engagement. During my interview with Daniel he told me about a life altering experience that continues to shape the work that he does. One day he was walking down our city's main street when he saw a woman so beautiful that it stopped him in his tracks.

He wanted to speak to this woman but couldn't muster up the words to say to her. He was in awe but couldn't do anything about it. He was paralyzed by her beauty.

According to Daniel, it was this stranger, whom he's never seen again, that made him want to make Reading a better place. He made a promise to himself that he would try his best to improve the city for this woman. Not only did Daniel see himself in her, but he was able to see everyone else in the community through her as well. Every man, woman, and child became this anonymous woman. This was a transformative moment in Daniel's life. Since then, he has gone on to raise scholarship funds for international college students and founded the community transformation organization, Barrio Alegria (www.barrioalegria.com).

After hearing Daniel's story, I began to wonder what it would take for everyone to have these transformational moments that empower us to help our community just a little bit more. How do we get to the point of wanting to put others before ourselves because we have a genuine Love Of Community? To help us get started I've listed a few actions that we can take:

- Shop locally and dine at local restaurants instead of chain restaurants
- Utilize your local farmers market
- Attend events in your city hosted by community members, non-profits, and local organizations
- Talk to your neighbors beyond surface level conversations

- Smile at a stranger
- Buy a piece of property and consider opening an establishment that will serve your community (book store, internet café, etc.)
- Buy a piece of artwork from your artist friend
- Make a commitment to only buy Christmas and birthday gifts from local small businesses
- Make a commitment to volunteer once per week at a nearby school
- Make a commitment to volunteer once per month at a local soup kitchen
- Deliver meals-on-wheels
- Spend time at an elderly home, rehab center, or hospital
- Organize a neighborhood clean-up
- Help an elderly person cross the street
- Check-in with older or lonely neighbors to make sure they are OK

What else can you do? Add to the list:

_____

_____

_____

STAY AT A HOSTEL

It was an unusually chilly January Miami night when I arrived at the hostel. I was sharing a room with five other people, a mix of both men and women. After checking-in and getting all of the payment business out of the way, I nervously opened the door to the room where I would be staying. To my surprise, I was greeted by a dark box about twice the size of my college dorm room. It was wider and a just a little longer than the rectangle that I shared with my roommate while at West Chester. There were three bunk beds in the room, two that sat parallel to one another along the wall to my left, and one directly in front of me on the far end of the room.

It couldn't have been later than 8:00 PM but it was pitch black with the exception of a few rays of neon light peeking through a window covered with blinds. My eyes were immediately drawn to a light illuminating from a tablet being held by a dark figure on the lower level of the first set of bunk beds. Not thinking, I immediately reached for the light switch. Before flicking the switch on, I quickly remembered that this room wasn't *my* room. The lights were off for a reason. One of my temporary roommates was asleep, and the other lay there lifeless, focusing her gaze only on the tablet screen. It was awkward.

I wanted to get out of that unfamiliar place as quickly as possible. I used the light from my cell phone screen to cut through the darkness so that I could clumsily get dressed. Then I left. Before leaving I checked my laptop at the front desk just in case I was in a room with someone in need of a new computer. As I exited the hostel and walked out into the South Beach night, I thought about how weird the whole experience was and questioned myself about whether I'd made the right decision by choosing to stay at this hostel for four nights.

It only took two days for me to determine that I made the right decision. I just needed time to get adjusted. You feel an overwhelming sense of community while lodging at a hostel. Your roommates need a place to stay for the least amount of money and must trust you just as much as you must trust them. Everyone just wants a positive experience that will allow them to get the most out of their stay. Your roommates might speak to you or they may just move about their business while leaving you to yours, and that's okay.

One of the best things about hostels is that they cultivate an atmosphere where people are encouraged to communicate and share with one another in a way that most of us don't in our ordinary lives. When a woman from Paris attempted to make herself breakfast and realized that she didn't have oil to fry her egg with, she politely asked my friend Demetrius and me if she could borrow our oil (Demetrius met me in Miami my second day at the hostel). We were happy to help her, and in return she gave us access to her tea and coffee.

After eating a big breakfast and experiencing what black folks like to call *the itus*, our Parisian friend's coffee provided the perfect pick me up when all we really wanted to do was take a nap under the sun as we sat poolside with our computers in our laps. This is what the Love Of Community chapter is about; connecting with people from all walks of life, sharing spaces, finding commonalities, and making the world just a little easier for one another – one interaction, kind gesture, or smile at a time.

By the third day at the hostel there was no need to check my laptop at the front desk or hide my cellphone whenever I left the room. I trusted the people in my new community and they trusted me. I willingly left my phone unattended in plain sight and I wasn't worried about anyone stealing it. Originally, once Demetrius arrived we were only going to utilize a mixed room dorm for one night. After that first night our plan was to move into a private room. Instead we opted to stay in the mixed dorm to save a few dollars. Sharing a space with strangers wasn't so bad after all. Because we altered our plans, we had to switch rooms. When we arrived at our new space we met a young, friendly guy named Pepa. In addition to being one of my best friends, Demetrius is a hip-hop artist who goes by T.O.P. (Check out his music: www.triumphoverpoverty.com). Pepa is also a hip-hop artist, from Japan. Of course we immediately connected with Pepa and plan to visit him once we make it to Japan on T.O.P.'s international tour (gotta speak it, or in this case, write it into existence!).

Pepa showed us a lot of love and even came out to see T.O.P. perform at *Miami Live*. Had we never had that hostel experience we would have never met Pepa, our new friend who I without a doubt believe that we will one day chill with in Japan.

The next time you go on vacation or when you think that you don't have enough money to take one, consider staying at a hostel. They're not for everyone, but there's tremendous value to be found in hostel life for those of us willing to give it a try.

TAKE A WALK

The streets of Reading, PA are enclosed by mountain terrain that becomes oil painting-like when rich hues of burgundy, army green, and mustard yellow emerge every autumn. The population is just shy of 88,000 with more than 70% of the residents identifying as Black, Hispanic or Latino. The pretzel city is the moniker that they've given us, although most people I know don't really subscribe to that identifier.

Even in one of the poorest cities in the country (*The New York Times* made it official in 2011 with the article "Reading, PA, Knew It Was Poor. Now It Knows Just How Poor.") there is beauty everywhere – in the trees that line the homes, in the Spanish and hip-hop music blasting from the cars, and in the faces of the residents – some more financially stable than others, and most feeling the perils of living in an urban dwelling that is trapped in poverty's grips.

A few years ago I lived in an apartment located within walking distance of everywhere I needed to be in the city. My red-brick building on Walnut Street between 8th and 9th streets stood erect in what felt to me like the middle of the city. While living here, I owned a car that was going to be out of commission for a few weeks. As I prepared to go car-less, I was looking forward to exploring my city by foot so that I could embrace its small-town but plausible energy in a way that I never had before.

One day while walking down one of my city's brick paved streets, I realized just how desensitized to my environment I was starting to become. Like most of us, I was so accustomed to driving around in my fast moving car that I had forgotten what it was like to commune with my community in this way. When things were slower and my attention wasn't occupied by the responsibility of driving and listening to whatever hip-hop or R&B music I was blasting at the time, I became more attuned to my surroundings. I started to notice that there was a lot more work to be done than I had originally thought. I knew that I lived in a poverty stricken city, but walking amongst the poverty as opposed to hastily driving past it changed my perspective. It made me want to do more and be more, for myself, and my community. But don't take my word for it, try it sometime; take an unnecessary walk around your city, town or neighborhood, and let that walk inspire you to embrace Love of Community in a new and exciting way.

Love Of Community

Chapter 3

LOVE OF KNOWLEDGE

Message In The Music:
"I N I"
by
Amel Larrieux

"Some people talkin' bout when judgment day will come
Looking down upon those not down with their religion
You must believe in all they say and all they do
And if you don't then heaven's gates are closed to you
I do not subscribe to their philosophy
I don't think my God wants them judgin' me
Followin' like I'm blind just won't do for me
God knows what's in my heart
That's why I gotta be
I n I"

Know
Don't just be on the ledge
Gather then distribute
That's how we get ahead
Learn
Then unlearn too
Grow
Water your garden
So that you'll always be in bloom
Seeds
Gift them with new presence
Then watch what they can do
Knowledge

I admire people who are thirsty for knowledge and can retain it and spit it out like a fire hydrant spewing ice cold water onto the summer bodies of kids in the projects. That's not quite me though. I'm the person who will look up Costa Rica on Wikipedia at the airport on the way to Costa Rica (true story). But this chapter isn't about how knowledgeable or not knowledgeable I am on any one subject. This chapter is about sharing information and personal stories that can help you on your journey to put love first and succeed at doing what you love.

I'll use this time to explore a few topics and practices that are often overlooked due to misinformation and religious intolerance. As with anything that is mentioned in this book, after reading and deciphering what the text means for you and your life, I encourage you to go out and do your own research. There's no way that I could advocate that you have a Love Of Knowledge without advising you to do this. My hope is that this chapter will spark your interest so that you can step out of your comfort zone and try something new or further explore a topic that I introduce to you. While you will find a few statistics, this chapter isn't about data and history. Everything that I write in this chapter (and in this book for that matter) is coming from a soul's place with the intent of connecting with your heart first and foremost.

CHURCH

When I'm walking among a sea of trees whose colors have changed due to the Universe's perfect plan, I am convinced that God is real. When I sit on a rock, uninterrupted, amongst a congregation of insects, I am reminded of God's mercy and unrelenting presence. No matter the weather or climate, when I am in nature I am both the church and the attendee. I've never felt like this in any building called church though, and I've been to quite a few of them.

When we hear the word "church" we think of a building where people of a similar faith congregate to worship. The Merriam-Webster definition reads: "A building used for public Christian worship." This is what most of us know church to be today in spite of the many rivaling meanings and origin of the word.

Despite contradicting definitions and verbiage that has been passed down, translated and manipulated for hundreds of years, we know in our heart of hearts what feels right, what brings us the most joy, and what actions, thoughts, and intentions will aid us in putting love first in all areas of our lives. As able bodies with sound minds, God has given us the ability to discern for ourselves what holds true to us and sits right with our souls. This is one of the reasons why I stopped attending church many years ago. It wasn't a place where I felt at home or that my spirit was being fed in the way that God intended it to be. There was too much performing, too much call and response, too many rituals, too many nice outfits, and too much judgement.

My relationship with church in the traditional sense started when I was in elementary school and attended a Spanish speaking church with my Aunt Gladys and my two brothers. The red building sat comfortably on the corner of 10th and Elm streets, across the street from the Genesius Theatre. I remember it being small and loud, but also inviting. At that time my brothers and I understood even less Spanish than we understand now, so .we couldn't comprehend anything that was said beyond Cumpleano Feliz (happy birthday) when the congregation would sing happy birthday to someone. My abuelo also attended that church and was proud to have his three half Black grandchildren there.

As a teenager I attended Spring Valley Church of God with my mom and brother Gil. My brother Nick may have been away at college or old enough to opt out of coming with us. The teen bible class wasn't bad and I enjoyed the music most of the time too. Whenever I knew that a dark haired Latina woman named Christina was about to sing I would wait with anticipation. Her powerful but controlled voice sent the congregation into a frenzy. She was the Whitney Houston of the church.

After attending Spring Valley for a year or two we became regulars and even got baptized there. At that time I didn't fully understand what it meant to be baptized and I didn't really question it either. I do remember my mother letting my brother and me decide for ourselves if we wanted to be baptized though. It seemed like the right thing to do so I did it even though I knew that taking a dip in the church's pool wouldn't stop me from cursing when I was around my friends, fighting with Gil, or having sex.

When I became an adult and began rethinking and then unlearning passed down traditions and trusting my God-gifted instinct, going to church became a different experience for me. My liberal arts education wouldn't allow me to not critically analyze Christianity and Spring Valley. I couldn't get down with the hollering and the crying either. And the passing out? Forget about it. The lack of people in leadership roles who looked like me and my family was a problem too. Yeah there was a row of flags representing many different countries that hung proudly above our heads as we walked into the sanctuary, but this United Nations wasn't reflected when I looked at the leaders of the church or when it was time to cast the roles of baby and adult Jesus in the Christmas play every year. When I thought about leadership at the church I thought about patriarchy. Every Sunday, Pastor Hinson, a white man, and gifted storyteller, preached to the diverse crowd of mostly Latinos, some of whom included my mom (my dad was not yet a Christian at this time), aunts, and uncles, then passed the baton down to his son. I often wondered what Sister Crawl, a Black woman, would preach about had she had the chance to share her wisdom with us in addition to sharing the church's announcements. Sister Crawl reminded me of the grandmother from *Family Matters*, the television sitcom that Steve Urkel's character made popular in the 90's. She's short and sweet, but doesn't take any mess either. I didn't know her well, but I knew that without saying a word, she could discipline me or love on me with her eyes alone. She gives great hugs too. These revelations (and others) combined with my quarrels with Christianity's role in enslaving my ancestors led me to seek out other methods of "having church."

Nowadays I aim to have church everywhere I go with everything that I do. When I am sitting at my desk using my writing talent I am having church. When I am packing gently worn clothes and canned goods to send to my family in Puerto Rico whose lives have been forever changed due to hurricane Irma, I am having church. When I am giving a young person advice I am having church. One of the Godliest acts we can undertake is to impart church into every part of our day, every day.

One of the best ways to feel God's love is to go chill in the woods surrounded by trees. Even better than this, do it barefoot. It's called grounding or earthing. Because there are more negative charges in the earth than there are in our bodies, when we walk barefoot on natural surfaces like grass or sand, we inhabit the earth's electrons resulting in a number of health benefits, including more energy and an increase in anti-inflammatory properties (*Journal of Alternative and Complementary Medicine*).

In addition to all of the health benefits associated with being outside in nature, like the Vitamin D that we get from the sun, which helps us maintain healthy immune systems, one of the greatest way to appreciate God's love is to breathe the fresh air and look up at the sheer beauty of the place that we are blessed to call home. Among other things, so many times, appreciating nature in this way has sparked my creativity and made me more grateful and happy to be alive.

Schedule your next time to get out in nature (go to church). I'm going to go for a walk, run, hike, bike ride on:

_____ at _____ AM/PM.

MEDITATION

Cross legged, I sat on the edge of my bed preparing to give mediation a try for the very first time. I didn't really know what I was doing but I had Russell Simmons there to guide me. Of course Russell wasn't actually in my bedroom with me, but I was following the instructions that he provided in his book, *Do You*. Just like he told me to, I began to breathe in and out while concentrating on my breath. I wasn't all the way sure what that meant, but I stuck with it. Mouth closed, I let my breath travel in and out of my nose intentionally inviting each breath in and then letting it go. A few long minutes passed. Before I knew it I was having my first out of body meditative experience. Floating. It felt as if I had levitated off of my full size mattress and made myself comfortable in the thin air that existed between my bed and the high ceiling of my apartment. Then tears began to well up in the corners of my eyes and fall lifelessly down my face. I thought about using my hands to wipe the moisture away but I chose to let it find its way down my cheeks and land where it wished.

In an attempt to be as "in the moment" as possible, I tried my best not to think about how my body felt or the fact that I was crying. It was a new feeling, but I wasn't afraid of it. I knew that this was a part of what I was "supposed" to be doing. I was taken aback by the magnitude of my first meditation experience, but I tried not to focus on that. I wanted to stay in my meditative state and stay out of my head as much as possible. With no real interpretation of time, I was suddenly interrupted by the chirping of my cell phone alarm indicating that twenty minutes had passed. When I opened my eyes I felt rested and energized. I knew that this wouldn't be my last time meditating. Although I've had other mind blowing meditations, my first meditation was momentous. It was like that initial high that people who use hard drugs experience after taking their very first hit – the high that they continue to chase but will never actually catch.

Meditation has since become an important part of my life. It is a companion that is there no matter what. It allows me to focus my energy and connect to my breath – my life Source – in a way that nothing else can. For someone making their best attempt to put love first and succeed at doing what they love, there really is no better tool than meditation. Whether for twenty-five minutes or five minutes, meditation will always be there waiting with open arms, serving as a beacon of light during the dark times that you encounter on your path. Not to mention, meditation has been medically proven to lower high blood pressure, relieve anxiety and depression, reduce stress, fight heart disease, improve focus, calm the nervous system, and help our immune systems function properly.

The ultimate goal of meditation (although it can vary for each individual) is to sit in silence without thinking about anything, which is admittedly easier said than done. But, with practice it gets easier. Meditation is something that you have to be willing to work at with no judgement tied to how good or bad you think you may be doing. Some days it's easy for me to slip into a meditative state, and on other days my mind travels everywhere but to a place of stillness. If you're a beginner sitting still for five minutes may feel like an eternity. You might find yourself thinking about trivial thoughts like what you will eat for lunch or if yesterday's outfit looked okay. If you're like me, your mind may drift off to some weird places. Whenever this happens simply direct your attention back to your breath and concentrate on being in the moment, breathing your way through each instance of your meditation.

By simply sitting in silence for an extended period of time you are meditating. Once you remember that there is no right or wrong way to meditate you will stop judging yourself about doing it correctly. Despite there not being a correct way to meditate, there are tools that you can use to enhance your practice. Here's one of them. The next time you're meditating and are having trouble staying in the present, take a deep breath. Before you let that breath out notice the instantaneous moment that exists after you inhale and before you exhale, that's the present. That's where you want to place your focus. Whenever you get distracted bring yourself back to that space. Here's another tip. Think of your thoughts as clouds and think of yourself as someone observing those clouds (thoughts). Try your best not to focus on any of them, just watch them float by. It's said that the space between thoughts (clouds) is where we hear God speak to us. When a thought or idea does pop into your head, say "thank you but no thank you" to yourself. By doing this you acknowledge the thought but don't attach yourself to it. This is the easiest way for me to continually bring my mind back to a place of stillness. With the upwards of fifty thousand thoughts that pop into our heads per day, and the fifty or so that pop into our heads per minute, learning to quiet our minds takes training.

Keep in mind that your meditation practice should be individual to you. Sometimes I start my meditation with a prayer and then move to a mantra, other times I listen to a guided meditation on YouTube or just sit in silence for twenty minutes. My favorite mantra at the moment is: "I am peace, light, and love. May all of my thoughts, actions, and interactions be grounded in peace, light, and love." Sometimes I repeat this silently and other times I concentrate on my breathing, in gratitude of the fact that I have breath. There's something special about calming my mind and breathing my way toward a better day and a better life. It brings me closer to where I need to be, spiritually and emotionally. Each time I treat myself to a few minutes of stillness I vibrate just a little bit higher.

There are a number of different ways to meditate. I like to I find the most quiet and peaceful spot in my apartment, whether it be my living room or my bedroom. Then I light sage and turn out the lights. If you're unfamiliar, the act of burning sage, or smudging as some people call it, is a spiritual cleansing ritual used by Native American and other indigenous people. The Native Americans would burn sage during ceremonies and use it to bring about healing. Today, people use sage to clear the energy in their homes and detoxify and purify the air (smoke from sage has been scientifically proven to remove bacteria from the air for up to 24 hours). After I light my sage I take my seat on the couch or on my bed, legs crossed, making sure that my back is supported so that I can sit up as straight as possible. I then place my hands on my knees. Most times I will leave my hands palms down to attract grounding energy. Every once in a while I will flip my hands over and leave them palms up. When I feel like I need to be grounded and focused it's palms down, if I'm feeling grounded going into the meditation then it's palms up, which puts me in more of a receiving state. Don't be afraid to switch back and forth between palms down and palms up during your meditation. I'm always amazed with how my energy shifts when I flip my hands from up to down or from down to up. While the idea is to sit motionless during your meditation, you don't have be as motionless as a statue. If you have an itch, scratch it. If you need to roll your shoulders back and fix your posture so you're more comfortable feel free to do that too.

Some people prefer a moving meditation like: running, coloring, or drawing. These forms of meditation are just as valuable as the method that I've mentioned. In his article, "Top Ten Meditation Raps: An Introspective Look," writer Adisa Banjoko breaks it down pretty simply. He writes: "Some meditate with the spoken word, others by writing with the pen or the paint brush. Some meditate to music, many meditate in complete silence. Stillness comes as it comes."

Only you can decide what style of meditation works best for you. If you've never meditated before, try it out and determine what feels good to you, whether it is something that resembles what I described, or a practice that doesn't involve sitting still at all. For many people, including myself, doing yoga is another form of meditation.

YOGA

*"Movement is medicine for creating change in
a person's physical, emotional, and mental states."*
– Carol Welch

I couldn't shake my feelings of uneasiness. Eyes closed, seated Indian style on my bed, I squirmed like a young child in the barber chair for his first time, in search of an inkling of familiar comfort so that I could meditate for twenty minutes. I couldn't find mental or physical stillness. I felt like my organs were desperately searching for a way to jump out of my skin. Then I started to have trouble breathing; I couldn't catch my breath or use it as a focal point like I usually do when I meditate. I started to panic; I didn't know why, but I was having an anxiety attack.

Before things got any worse I jumped out of bed and onto the floor into the downward dog position that I'd done so many times in yoga class. Butt in the air, palms and feet planted firmly on the floor I moved from that upside down 'V' position into a sun salutation three times. I focused on my breath and matched my breathing to my movements. After three minutes all of the uncomfortable and anxious feelings that I felt subsided. Thankfully, this has only happened to me one other time. I am even more grateful that if it were to happen again I know exactly what to do.

In 2013, *The Hindustan Times* reported that there are over 200 million people worldwide practicing yoga. Over 100 million of those people reside in India, the country where Yoga originated. With over 7 billion people in the world, there's still a lot of work to be done to spread the good news about yoga.

I was introduced to yoga a few years ago by a good friend of mine named Rochelle. Rochelle was in the beginning stages of yoga teacher training and needed someone to practice on, so I was that person (she now has her own yoga company, *Creative Mindz Yoga*, www.creativemindzyoga.com). Being completely honest, I didn't immediately fall in love with yoga. It was a process that took time. After my initial lesson with Rochelle, I began using yoga videos on YouTube before eventually taking classes that my part-time job offered. These days I practice several times a week. On more than one occasion I've used it to energize me, calm my nerves, start my day, make my day better and gain clarity. It has undoubtedly been one of the best ways for me to connect with God's infinite love and wisdom.

Yoga calms the nervous system, helps your immune system, and improves joint function. And these are just a few of the benefits. There are far too many to list them all here. In addition to the health benefits, for me yoga serves as a constant reminder to stay aligned with my life Source by breathing through every obstacle that presents itself in my life. Every time we do yoga we literally put ourselves in difficult positions that we have no choice but to breathe our way through. Once you begin practicing regularly you'll find that you'll begin to breathe your way through difficult positions when you're not in a yoga class too (not to mention, it's pretty cool that first time you unexpectedly use your yoga skills in the bedroom, but that's a topic for another book). It will be subtle, but you'll start to notice that the next time you're in traffic or in an unnecessarily long check-out line at the supermarket, instead of getting frustrated you will find your breath and look for the pieces of positivity that can be found in every situation. Before you know it, yoga will gently make its way into all areas of your life whether you invite it to or not – it's that kind of friend.

We're living, breathing entities that can change our moods by simply changing our thoughts and the positioning of our bodies. If I didn't have the principles of yoga to calm me down and help me see things clearly, I'm not sure what I would do. This proved to be true a few days ago when I found an unexpected guest in my home. I was making my way down the steps to my apartment when I turned the corner to find a garden snake just chillin' on my floor like he owned the place. It scared the shit out of me. I jumped back and immediately began looking for a weapon so that I could end this snake's life. I glanced at a large book sitting on an end table to my left, but that wouldn't work. Although this snake was a trespasser in my home, it didn't deserve to die like this, and I wasn't convinced that my book would do the job anyway. I also didn't want snake guts on my new book about India. While I was contemplating which weapon to use and evaluating my life as a man afraid of a small snake, my visitor was gliding around my apartment, looking for a place to hide from the scared human dancing around it. I needed to find my breath.

As usual, when I stopped to breathe I was able to calm myself down and think rationally. No longer scared, I decided that the first thing that I needed to do was locate the snake. The last thing that I wanted was for it to get out of my sight for good. If I let that happen I knew the thought of it popping up unannounced would haunt me until it slithered back into my sight again. So I kept looking around my apartment until I found it. With just its small head peeking out, I spotted it hiding underneath a decorative basket that sits under a wooden end table in my living room. Now what? I grabbed my other decorative basket and politely coerced the small snake out from underneath the first basket into the one that I was holding. I had it. Carefully, I watched it coyly slide around the bottom of the basket as I quickly walked it outside and set it free in my backyard. As I made my way back into my apartment I had to smile and take a moment of gratitude for yoga. Once again it helped me find my breath and think rationally. With or without the aid of a reptile, yoga continues to remind me to always come back to my breath, my life force. It serves as a constant reminder that very rarely are things as serious or as permanent as we like to believe they are.

YOU'RE A MIRACLE, NOT A SINNER

We're not born into sin. The fact that we're born at all makes us miracles. Think about that. Treat yourself like you know that you're a miracle. You're not a sinner trying to get it right, you're a miracle who is both right and "wrong" and can embrace and accept all that that entails. To accept that we were born into sin places us comfortably in a position to believe that we've been "wrong" since birth, that from the very beginning there was something about our nature that needed to be fixed and made better. I can't believe this even if I tried. Have you ever watched a baby move about a room without a care in the world other than to express love to themselves and the people around them? Babies are joy in its most unadulterated human form. For me, there may be no more perfect being than a baby (a miracle). It's now time to change the narrative. Let's teach our children that they were born out of love and into perfection so that they can treat themselves and others as if they're fully aware of their true worth.

HEAVEN & HELL

*"Who was King James? And why did he think it was
so vital to remove chapters and make his own version of
the Bible? They say Hell is underground and Heaven is
in the sky, that's where you go when you die,
but how they know?"*
– Talib Kweli

Sakyong Mipham opens his book *Ruling Your World* with a story about visiting his friends Adam and Allie and their two-year-old son Javin. He writes about how his friends were impressed by their son's ability to naturally know certain ways of being without having to be taught them. He then goes on to explain the concept of "basic goodness," which he defines as innate wisdom. Mipham writes: "Our minds are vast and profound. In his teachings on rulership, this innate wisdom is known as 'basic goodness.' It is the natural, clear, uncluttered state of our being. We are all appointed with heaven – great openness and brilliance. Bringing this heaven down to earth, into our daily life, is how we rule our world."

Like Mipham, I believe that every day is a new opportunity to bring a state of heaven into our lives. Doing what we innately know is right, while trying our best to live our truth is heavenly. Loving ourselves and those around us is heaven. To hate what you do for a living is hell. Being forced to act and behave a certain way to avoid a place called hell is also hell. Heaven and hell are right now; states of mind, not physical places. When we live with purpose and proactively seek out ways to be more loving to ourselves and others, we're in heaven. When we're not doing this, we're in Hell. It's really that simple. We don't need to go back and forth about whether or not hell is mentioned in the old testament of the bible or if it's even a real place. What's most important is that we make a concerted effort to produce new moments of experiencing heaven every day that we have the privilege of being alive.

Most of us were not taught as children that we can establish heaven on earth when we honor God by doing what we love. As people who make love our religion, it's our responsibility to take ownership of the heaven and hell narrative because it's not loving enough. By changing the narrative we change our perspective. Once our perspectives change our actions and our outlook changes too. I should've been told as a child that I had the power to bring heaven into my life. Instead I was told that if I sinned and didn't accept a man as my savior then I was going to a fiery place under the ground called hell (despite the fact that the earth is a spinning ball in the universe).

TRY SOMETHING NEW: CHANTING IN NYC

We arrived at SGI Cultural Center in Manhattan not far from Union Square in the early evening of a cold fall day. Happy to be out of work and the frigid

Manhattan temperature, my friend Sophia, my co-worker Bryan and I entered the building and were immediately greeted by a friendly front desk attendant. After Sophia, a practicing Buddhist and member of the Cultural Center, signed Bryan and me in as her guest we made our way to the elevator. I was out of my comfort zone but I somehow knew that I was in for an emotional and enlightening experience.

The first room that we arrived at was packed to the brim with "advanced chanters." "Nam-myoho-renge-kyo, Nam-myoho-renge-kyo, Nam-myoho-renge-kyo" they chanted feverishly. Everyone was reciting the words in unison with their eyes fixed toward an alter at the front of the room that I later learned is called a butsudan. Realizing that this might be too much for Bryan and me, Sophia suggested that we go to a less crowded room where the chanting was being done at a slower pace. Once we found our new room we quietly made our way to the front and found seats in the first row of gold chairs accented with soft cherry red cushions.

It was unlike anything I'd ever seen. It was obvious that there was worshipping going on but it wasn't any type of worshiping that I had seen before. There was no one standing at the front of the room preaching or giving instructions. There was no collection plate and no one was dressed fancily either. The crowd was diverse in both nationality and age and paid no mind to one another. Everyone seemed to be focused on their chanting. It was as if they were worshipping themselves.

I felt a bit out of my element, but I was ready to chant in the same way that everyone else was chanting. Once I made myself comfortable in my seat I let out a timid "Nam-myoho-renge-kyo," somewhat embarrassed by the sound of my nasally voice. Then I said it again, this time a little louder. I had the saying down but I was off beat (which was very disappointing to my Blackness). After a few tries I was in rhythm with everyone else in the room. I didn't like the idea of keeping my eyes open though. Unlike the other chanters, I chose to close my eyes instead of staring at the butsudan. I wanted to focus my energy inward. "Nam-myoho-renge-kyo" I chanted over and over again as I slipped into what felt like a very aware and active meditation.

Similar to the way that I got emotional the first time that I meditated, I began to cry while chanting. I wasn't sure why I was crying and I wasn't interested in exploring the reason either. I just kept chanting as my mind and body moved closer and closer to stillness despite all of the chanting from the other people around me. When I opened my eyes I felt an overwhelming sense of peace. It was a feeling I often associate with meditation, but there was something different about this peace that I can't quite describe. It was amplified and distributed throughout my entire body. I felt lighter. I had let go of the weight of emotions that had stored themselves away in the crevices of my being.

Chanting has since become a regular part of my meditation practice. Sometimes I'll chant while meditating and I almost always end a silent meditation with a few minutes of chanting. By doing this I'm declaring my faith in Mystic Law and the belief that life's possibilities are endless. Buddhist philosopher, educator, and author, Daisaku Ikeda describes Mystic Law as: "the unlimited strength inherent in one's life." According to Ikeda, to believe in the Mystic Law and chant is an act of faith in our unlimited potential. He writes: "It is not a mystical phrase that brings forth supernatural power, nor is Nam-myoho-renge-kyo an entity transcending ourselves that we rely upon. It is the principle that those who live normal lives and make consistent efforts will duly triumph. To chant Nam-myoho-renge-kyo is to bring forth the pure and fundamental energy of life, honoring the dignity and possibility of our ordinary lives."

Had I not been willing to give chanting a try I would have never discovered this serene way to focus my energy and enhance my meditations. Does this make me a Buddhist? Not at all. When you choose love as your religion you're open to trying a number of different practices so that you can discover which ones feel most authentic to you and your journey.

YOU ARE WHAT YOU EAT: GIVE YOURSELF LIFE

Similar to a high performance car that needs quality fuel, your body needs the proper nutrients for it to operate at its peak. I'm not a healthcare professional and I won't bore you with a lot of data but I will remind you that food either gives us life or brings us closer to death. There's really no in between. When you choose food that gives you life you honor yourself and your body's natural ability to heal itself and function properly. If we expect to move throughout the day with vigor and energy, we have to be mindful about what we're eating.

The more alkaline our bodies are the better they can fight disease and help keep us healthy and happy. By eating more nutrient rich leafy greens, vegetables, fruits, and legumes, and less dairy, soy, and caffeine we have the potential to change the PH balance of our bodies. When we do this we experience better sleep and increased energy, as well as a host of other benefits. According to the late renowned herbalist, Dr. Sebi, who's most known for curing cases of HIV and cancer, a plant based diet that is plentiful in nutrient rich food is the best way to eliminate mucus in the body that has the potential to lead to disease. Dr. Sebi, along with many other holistic healthcare professionals believe that disease cannot exist in an alkaline environment, that our bodies were made to heal themselves when we eat the right "life giving" foods. While there are health professionals who argue against this philosophy, it is one that I've chosen to adopt because it makes the most sense for me. Although I do, on rare occasions, eat small amounts of meat and dairy.

We weren't taught that food is our medicine, that we can take control of our gut health, our mental state, and our immune systems by eating the right foods and drinking drinks like natural kefir water, raw kombucha, and organic apple cider vinegar. This is why I wanted to include this information in this chapter. Once we have this knowledge we can put it to use and begin showing ourselves love in this way. It's not about making drastic changes to your diet either. You can make small changes like swapping from white sugar to brown sugar, from regular milk to coconut milk, and minimizing the amount of meat you consume on a daily basis.

Most of us have been conditioned to think that we're supposed to have meat with every meal although two sides of vegetables and a starch will fill us up just the same. Part of having a Love Of Knowledge is moving away from this type of conditioning. For example, we were also conditioned to believe that milk is the best source of calcium, but now we have learned otherwise. We know that kale, oats, white beans, chia seeds, bok choy, and almonds all have more calcium in them than milk.

What are three small changes that you can make to your diet so that you can treat your body in a more loving way?

1. _____

2. _____

3. _____

WOMEN

"Y'all don't treat women fair / She read about herself in the bible, believing she the reason sin is here / You played her, with an apron / Like, 'Bring me my dinner, dear' / She the nigger here."
– Nas

More often than not when we learn about stories in the bible we usually do one of two things – take these stories with a grain of salt, or believe them as absolute truths without questioning or researching the source or the intention behind them. Luckily, we have prophets like Nas to give us an opposing perspective. To Nas's point, when you think of sin, what comes to mind? More often than not we think of negativity and evil, living in a way that is unjust or wrong. When we willingly subscribe to the idea that women are the cause of sin we make an unnecessary and ungodly connection between women and negativity, women and subordination, women and the opposite of everything that is good. We might even think of death, which is strangely ironic being that women are the only human portals of life. Why did the authors of the Genesis chapter choose to write the story this way? While we may not have all of the answers, ideologies aside, we know whether or not this feels good to our souls. We can answer for ourselves if these notions are loving and Godly or if they are divisive and discriminatory.

Throughout history, whether by class, race or faith, women have been treated as second class citizens. This happens in every part of the world, despite women being more vital to the continued existence of humanity than anything else. Sadly, these direct and covert attacks against women have worked well and continue to perpetuate inequality in 2018. For example, it's still not the norm for a female to be at the head of a Christian church or sit in the presidential seat in the United States. And women are still paid less than men to do the same exact jobs. According to the World Bank Gender Data Poll, women in most countries earn on average 60-75% of men's wages. But the tides are slowly changing because the ways of the past won't work for the future. Research firm, Barna Group reports that female pastors are on the rise. Their research states that one of out of every 11 Protestant pastors is a woman, triple the amount as a century ago.

As I sit here writing this section I try to imagine what it might feel like to belong to the group who "created sin." I don't get very far, but I know that it doesn't feel good. As a society, I don't think we've taken the time to analyze and digest how problematic these accusations are for both men and women, not to mention little boys and girls. If you're a woman or girl reading this, let this be a tender but firm reminder that you are a Goddess – the core of the holy trinity that is man, woman, child – don't let any man or belief system tell you otherwise, and certainly don't let it dictate how you go about creating success in your life.

Chapter 4
LOVE OF CELEBRITY LIFE

Message in the Music:

"Vivir Mi Vida"
by
Marc Anthony

"Voy a reír, voy a bailar
Pa' qué llorar, pa' que sufrir
Empieza a soñar, a reír
Voy a reír (oho!), voy a bailar
Siente y baila y goza
Que la vida es una sola
Voy a reír, voy a bailar
Vive, sigue
Siempre pa'lante, no mires pa'trás
Eso! mi gente
La vida es una"

Both imagined and lived
Here and now
Void of pretense and glamour
It's a lifestyle
Given unto self
Not filthy
Maybe rich
With or without wealth
It sees no limits
It's present and it's future
And it's for the now
It knows that possibilities are endless
So it doesn't question how
Just love
Just celebrity
Minus flashing lights
It could be yours
It could be heavenly
It's Love
Of
Celebrity
Life

The first time that I let myself believe that I was a celebrity it was only in my head. After I decided to fully commit to being a writer I started to live the life of a celebrity writer. I frequented as many events as possible and covered those events as if they were the biggest things going on in the entertainment industry. When I attended a fashion show at The Bollman Center at Albright College, in my mind I was at New York Fashion Week on assignment for *The New York Times*. In reality, I wasn't on assignment for anyone. I wrote the story (without pay) as a citizen journalist for a local non-profit publication. It didn't matter though. The vibrational frequency of my thoughts that were being projected into the Universe was what was most important. Everything starts in the mind. While sitting in that gymnasium watching the volunteers walk across a makeshift runway, I was grateful to be living out a small piece of my dream.

Fast forward one year later, the seed that I planted grew into the reality that I wanted it to be. As I stood amongst the other fashion enthusiasts surrounded by graffiti tagged walls in a dimly lit rectangular room, I couldn't help but be proud of myself. I was at New York Fashion Week in Midtown Manhattan attending a show hosted by Jeantrix, a designing duo out of Philadelphia who've dressed everyone from Alicia Keys to Beyoncé's already famous daughter, Blue Ivy. The room was overflowing with bloggers, media personalities, and fashion lovers of all kinds.

*****

Love of Celebrity Life is about inhabiting the work ethic and ambition to pursue your dreams the way that celebrities pursue their dreams. Celebrities live great lives. I'm not talking about a celebrity's private life, or their mental health, I'm talking about their day-to-day activities. I'm talking about the vacations, the personal trainer, the nice homes, the charitable donations, the vegan food, and the yoga classes. I'm talking about the best of everything, in a way that feels most authentic to you.

Let's be clear though. I'm not suggesting that to live a happy life you need to live extravagantly, take luxurious trips, and eat the finest foods. What I am suggesting is that you have the ability and talent to live this way if this is what you desire. Living a celebrity lifestyle helps me live my best life and remain steadfast in pursuit of the goals that I wish to accomplish. Despite this, I'm well aware of the fact that taking trips and accumulating money will not give me a happy and successful life. I know that money and travelling can't do this. Only I can do this for myself.

When I spent nine days in Costa Rica at a writing retreat (more on this later) I lived a very simple life. My un-air conditioned bungalow was perfect. In lieu of a living room, my bed greeted me as soon as I opened the door. There was a wash area adjacent to the bed, a small bathroom to the left of that, and a kitchen. That's it. There were no fancy decorations, high-tech gadgets, or anything that resembled modernity, but I loved my simple villa. When I returned home to my carefully decorated apartment, accented with bold bursts of burgundy, navy blue, and mustard yellow, I realized how little having a beautiful home actually means in the grand scheme of things. Sure, I appreciate the fact that my apartment is comfortable and pleasing to the eye, but my villa in Costa Rica was just as special. We are at our best when we're fulfilled and satisfied living at either end of the spectrum. Both experiences are valuable. Whether an extravagant mansion tucked away in the Hollywood hills, or a modest home in a place like New Orleans, having a Love Of Celebrity Life is realizing that we can live exactly how we want to live wherever we want to live.

It's important to mention that what may be lavish or abundant for one person may be totally different for another person. For example, let's say there's a school teacher who lives in a nice home with a spouse who makes a similar salary. If these two people can dine out as they wish, give back to worthy causes, and take one or two vacations per year, this is their version of living a celebrity life. This is especially true if they love what they do for a living.

Embracing a Love Of Celebrity Life is a mindset more than anything else. You don't have to go to the spa to have a spa day. You can create a spa environment without having to leave the comfort of your own home. Light a few candles, put on some soothing music and run yourself a bath. And as the warm water wrinkles your skin, you can use your mind to project yourself to the fanciest spa in Beverly Hills if this is the type of spa experience you'd like to attract. By doing this you're inviting the Universe to work with you to give you exactly what you want.

TAKE RISKS

Celebrities take risks. Whether it be a female rapper like Queen Latifah venturing into film, modeling, and hosting a daytime television show, or someone like Jennifer Lopez who started out as a backup dancer and now stars in and produces television shows, celebrities trust themselves and their abilities. You have to do the same thing.

I take risks with my time and money often. For example, for six years I was the senior editor of an independent magazine started by a friend of mine and one of his childhood friends. We poured hundreds of dollars and hours into the project, and loved every minute of it. When I stopped loving it, even though I realized that my dream of blowing the magazine up to the capacity that I still know that it can reach was realistic, I stopped doing it. Some would say that I wasted my time and my money, but that couldn't be further from the truth. The knowledge that I gained is invaluable. From learning how to manage a staff of writers to conducting my first celebrity interview, every situation provided nuggets of experience and wisdom that continue to contribute to who I am as a writer and entrepreneur.

I can remember anxiously waiting for legendary hip-hop artist and businessman Styles P of The Lox to arrive at the studio. It was my first celebrity interview. When his black Porsche Cayenne with peanut butter leather guts pulled up outside, it was showtime. I needed to be on my A-game and I couldn't let my nerves get the best of me. I had listened to his latest album, *Super Gangster (Extraordinary Gentleman)*, from top to bottom and I was prepared to ask him thought provoking questions that I knew his fans would appreciate. I learned two valuable lessons during that interview. I learned that people enjoy hearing themselves talk and that Styles P doesn't like to share his blunts. After that I went on to interview a then up-and-coming Philly rapper named Meek Mill, international superstar Maya Azucena, veteran emcee Cormega, Bronx spitter, Joell Ortiz, and a few other notable artists. Each one provided me with valuable insight about their careers, which in turn added enormous value to mine.

*****

A few months ago I risked a whole day's worth of time and $74.00 to attend a publishing event hosted by Art Sanctuary, a non-profit arts organization in Philly.

I know what you're thinking. $74.00 isn't a lot of money. You're right. And it's especially not a lot of money if you live by the principles that I outline in the Love Of Money chapter. However, when you're a writer and an early stage entrepreneur without a full-time job, $74.00 is $74.00. But there was something telling me that I needed to be at this event.

When you're trying to figure out whether or not to take a risk (even a small $74.00 risk) you have to listen to your instinct and that God voice that will never steer you wrong. Because I wasn't afraid to risk money and my time, my trip to Philly turned out to be more than worth the price of my small investment. The publishing workshop provided me with a lot of useful information, and I also met Cristen and James, two people who are still a part of my life today. Cristen is a dancer involved in the arts and non-profit community, and James is a veteran writer and scholar who's been helping me with the primary components of writing and publishing this book. These blessings would have never shown themselves to me had I not made the decision to risk a little bit of my time and money.

LIVE YOUR PASSION & LOOK GOOD DOING IT

In high school I could go for one full month without wearing the same shirt. Every night before I went to sleep I would write down what clothing I wore to school each day so that I was never a repeat offender. It seems silly and materialistic now, but in hindsight I believe it to be more than that. None of our interests are given to us by accident. The Universe knew that as an adult I would further explore my appreciation for clothing by styling photo shoots and writing for fashion websites.

Because I often write about fashion, dressing nicely is important to the work that I do as a writer. When you're doing what you love you find ways to incorporate that love into every aspect of your life. This is how you live and breathe your work. If you're a hair stylist or a makeup artist your hair and makeup should always be on point. Doing this allows you to turn yourself into a walking, talking billboard for your talent.

When you look good, you feel good. You've heard this more times than you can count, but it really is true. Feeling good is one of the keys to happiness and success because feeling good aligns with thinking positively. When you feel good and you're thinking positively there's nothing that you can't do or accomplish.

"It was all a dream
I used to read Word Up Magazine"
– Notorious B.I.G.

VISION BOARDS & THE LAW OF ATTRACTION

The Notorious B.I.G had an impeccable vision for his future. He conveyed this vision with such clarity and surreal imagery on his lead single "Juicy" that it catapulted him into hip-hop superstardom and made him a hero to kids all over the world. For those three minutes or so he is a preacher at the pulpit prophesizing about what life is and could be over a sample of Mtume's "Juicy Fruit." Biggie wrote the predictive lyrics to "Juicy" long before MTV or mainstream radio knew who or what a Biggie Smalls was. Despite this, he spends the better half of the song rapping about a life that was only available to him in his mind. He spits:

"Condo in Queens/ Indo for weeks/ Sold out seats to hear
Biggie Smalls speak/ Livin' life without fear/
Puttin' five karats in baby girl's ear/
Lunches, brunches/ Interviews by the pool/
Considered a fool cause I dropped out of high school"

B.I.G. knew exactly what he wanted. He felt it. He made the Universe feel it too, and as a result the Universe collaborated with him to make his vision a reality. Although we may not have the skills to rap like Biggie, we can partner with the Universe the same way that he did. One way we can do this is by creating a vision board, a visual representation of what we want our lives to look like. Here's how you can do it.

To make a vision board you'll need a piece of cardboard or construction paper, glue, scissors, and a few old magazines. An imagination, a solid work ethic, and unwavering faith will help too. Next you'll need to look through the magazines and cut out words and pictures that represent the lifestyle that you wish to acquire. Then paste those images on your cardboard. Once it's finished place your vision board somewhere where you can see it every day and look at it with focused intention. Dedicate a few minutes to being creative with it too. If you have a picture of a swimming pool on your vision board imagine the temperature and pressure of the water cascading against your tanned body as you dive in headfirst. If you have a car on your board breathe in that distinct new car smell while you gaze at the picture with genuine excitement. And if you have the words "family" and "community" on your board (like I do) feel those feelings of family bonding and community companionship as you work together with your vision board to manifest a life that you can't live without.

I try to make one or two vision boards per year, and when I use them as a teaching tool with the high school students that I work with, I'm always impressed by how involved and imaginative they get with their boards. I usually use this time to make one for myself as well. I remember one year in particular when my vision board helped me to attract a car, a laptop, and a summer teaching position. This is how it went down. I wanted a new car so I placed a picture of a burgundy Chrysler on my board. I also wanted a Mac laptop computer so I put a picture of that on my board too. Another thing I put on my board was an image of a teacher and I wrote the words "college professor" above his head. I made this board in September. By the following June I had acquired an older model white Mac laptop and a summer teaching position with Upward Bound at Reading Area Community College. Because I would be working for Upward Bound as both a teacher and an advisor, I was responsible for transporting students to and from the program using a rental car. Imagine the smile on my face when I arrived at the rental car place only to find that the car that I would be using for the summer was the same make, model, and color as the picture of the car that I placed on my vision board a few months prior.

One thing to remember about vision boards is that they may not give you exactly what you want, exactly how you want it. This doesn't mean that they don't "work." When I placed a picture of a car on my vision board I wanted to own the car that I would be attracting into my life. The one that I got I had to give back at the end of the summer and could only use during work hours. And the summer teaching position that I attracted wasn't exactly a college professor teaching position, but I was teaching on a college campus nonetheless. It was also the first summer that I had been asked to teach a class for Upward Bound. And the Mac laptop that I attracted I bought for $200 from someone who was selling an old model that they didn't want anymore. It wasn't the best investment though because there was something wrong with the screen that prohibited me from using it not long after I bought it. But whether or not I made a smart investment isn't the point. The point is that intention, manifestation, and visualization are real. Better yet, the Law Of Attraction is real. Whether you're writing lyrics about the celebrity life you wish to obtain, or creating a vision board about it, you're using the Law Of Attraction. The law states that like attracts like, that our thoughts create a frequency and that frequency is then sent out into the Universe to attract a similar frequency.

According to Rhonda Byrne, author of *The Secret*, everyone from Plato to Shakespeare and Einstein were aware of the Law Of Attraction. She writes: "The law of attraction is the law of creation. Quantum physicists tell us that the entire Universe emerged from thought! You create your life through your thoughts and the law of attraction, and every single person does the same. It doesn't just work if you know about it. It has always been working in your life and every other person's life throughout history. When you become *aware* of this great law, then you become *aware* of how incredibly powerful you are, 'to be able to THINK your life into existence.'"

When I realized this it changed my life. In fact, Rhonda Byrne's *The Secret* changed my life. It was the summer of 2011, and I was in Philly with one of my best friends' Joey, to see *Beats, Rhymes, & Life: The Travels of a Tribe Called Quest*, a documentary film directed by Michael Rapaport, about legendary hip-hop group, A Tribe Called Quest. The film wasn't showing in Reading so we took a trip to a movie theater in Philly to watch it. As we drove up Market Street looking for a parking spot we passed a used bookstore neatly tucked away on a cobble-stone street not far from the theater. After finding parking we decided to check out the bookstore until it was time to go to see the movie. I don't remember the name of it, but it was one of those perfectly unkempt bookstores with an owner who lives and breathes books and has been collecting them for longer than you've been alive.

Once we were inside, Joey made his way up to the second floor in search of a book to buy for his mom and I stayed on the first floor perusing the collection of hardcover and paperback goodness. There were books everywhere, protruding off of shelves, piled high on the floor, and pushed into corners – all waiting to be adopted and taken to a new home. As I made my way toward a tall raggedy wooden bookshelf a few feet directly in front of the entrance I noticed that there was one book on the shelf that did not have its spine facing outward. Instead, this book's subtle, but intriguing cover design jumped out at me and grabbed my attention with all of its force. It stared me in the face and convinced me to approach it and start a conversation, so I did. I picked it up and began paging through it and checked the price. I don't remember if it was $15.00, but I do remember thinking that I've bought shirts for less than what this book cost. It seemed interesting but I wasn't convinced. I closed this book titled *The Secret*, put it back on the shelf and made my way upstairs to find Joey. After looking around for a few more minutes it was time to make our way to the movie theater. But before we left I had to buy *The Secret*. The Universe was telling me that I needed to have it. It was as if there was some type of magnetic power that was pulling me closer to it. I couldn't leave the bookstore without buying it and once I began reading it I understood why. *The Secret* changed my entire perspective. It made me realize that I am the master of my own fate and that my mind and thoughts are more powerful than I ever thought they were. It made me more mindful of my thoughts and how these thoughts help to construct my life.

List three things that you would like to attract into your life:

1._____

2._____

3._____

Chapter 5
LOVE OF MONEY

Message In The Music:

"Curry Chicken"
by
Joey Bada$$

"You got to give to get and then give back
You got to give to get and then give back
You got to give to get and then give back
Then you give back, then you, then you give back"

What you think about money?
You know what you think about money
It's only a piece of paper when we really think about
money
Think about sunny
Days and cold nights
Without heat
We were raised close tight
Oven door open
It's a universal theme
When the trouble's on
We voltron
Then we get the C.R.E.A.M.
That's what we think about money
What you think about money?
You know what you think about money
That's right
It's only a piece of paper when we really think about
money

The flight attendant was giving us special instructions but I couldn't understand why no one was paying attention to her. The middle-aged white woman wanted us to know that there was an oxygen mask that would drop down from an overhead compartment to save our lives if necessary. As she pointed to the exits I followed her hand gestures meticulously. "That exit is there, there's one right behind me too," I thought to myself. "Got it."

Before this, I naively assumed that everyone aboard an airplane paid attention to the flight attendant's safety demonstration. I was seventeen, on my way to Australia with thirty-five of my peers and two chaperones. It was a six hour flight to California, followed by a fourteen hour flight to Australia. Andrew was the only kid from my high school. All of the other students were from various high schools throughout Berks County. I was the only Latino and the only Black kid on the trip. My first flight didn't make me nervous, but, like my father always is, I was aware of my surroundings.

As we ascended into the sky I remember being surprised at how loud the plane roared and how fast it took off. Then time stood still as we cut through clouds on our way to California. I was too young and detached from my feelings to realize it at the time, but I was flying, literally and figuratively, for the first time in my life.

Traveling to Australia as a teenager opened me up to a world that was much bigger than anything that I had seen or experienced in Pennsylvania. I walked the Sydney Harbor Bridge as a burnt orange sun set behind me, swam in the Great Barrier Reef, and got pissed on while holding a koala bear. I wasn't sure how I would make it happen, but from that summer on I knew that I wanted my life to be filled with adventures like these. But to see the world in this way would require money. In this case, a little over $5,000.

Although the trip was expensive for my parents and their lower middle class income, the cost of the trip was never an issue. As my mom and I sat in the auditorium of an unfamiliar high school, in a foreign part of town, representatives from the People To People program told us how great the experience would be and how taking this trip to Australia was a once in a lifetime opportunity.

My parents weren't in the position to just write me a check, but there was never any question of whether or not we would get the money. We believed that it would happen and got to work. We solicited donations from local businesses and my mom sold her delicious pumpkin bread to anyone who would buy a loaf. Her church also took up a collection for me. We partnered with Bailey's Cheesesteak to do a sandwich fundraiser, and my ten aunts and uncles on my dad's side gifted me a joint donation as well. This combined with my parent's contribution and money I earned working part-time at Stride Rite shoe store made it possible for me to take the trip.

Accumulating the funds that took me to Australia gave me my first chance to use the power of belief to attract money into my life. It wouldn't be the last time that I would use it though. When I realized that money was an energy like everything else in life, I began to use it as such.

"If your intention isn't aimed at the highest good, having all of the money in the world still won't make you rich."

INTENTION

A few months ago I facilitated a workshop for a group of fellow writers. During the workshop I gave brief descriptions of the chapters in this book and answered questions about my writing process. Afterward, a friend of mine who attended told me that someone made a comment to him about me not having things "figured out" because I've included a chapter about money in a book about love. In this person's defense, I didn't go into too much detail about this chapter during my talk. I only mentioned that my life work includes helping as many people as possible, and that acquiring wealth will help me do this. What I didn't address, that is so important in terms of developing wealth, is intention.

Once I'm wealthy enough, I plan to help my family in ways that I've not been able to, and invest money into my community by funding initiatives and individuals who have a genuine interest in improving the quality of life for my city's residents. When it comes to gaining any kind of wealth, the reason you want to gain it is much more important than actually gaining it. Who do you want to help? How can your wealth benefit your community? Intention is essential. Will you create a scholarship in your name? Do you intend to have the means to afford the best healthcare for someone in your family battling a debilitating illness? How will your resources help as many people as possible? Maybe you'll use your money to only support eco-friendly businesses and purchase a fossil-fueled car so that you can help reduce pollution.

What types of causes will you help champion once you've acquired the amount of money that you desire? Write a few of them down here:

_____

_____

_____

In *Creative Mind and Success*, a fascinating book by Ernest Holmes, he explores intention in relation to giving. He writes: "There is no reason why a person should ever stop. This does not mean that we should be miserly, trying to accumulate more and more to hold, but that our thought should so enlarge that it cannot help gathering more and more, even though, on the other hand, or with the other hand, we are ever distributing that which we gather. Indeed, the only reason, for having is that we may give out of that which we have."

Like Holmes, I believe that, while having money is great, even more valuable is to have clear intentions on how you plan to help others once you have it. To receive more is to give more away. If you're looking to acquire wealth so that you can feel better about yourself, then you're pursuing riches for the wrong reasons.

*****

Many of us have been taught that money is the root of all evil because we've seen it ruin friendships and dismantle families. In spite of this and how we may feel about money, most of us want more of it. Luckily, everyone reading this book has the ability to use their talents to earn a substantial income and live an abundant life. These talents don't have to be related to singing, dancing, or sports either. For many of you these gifts include decorating a home, giving a healing massage, or teaching someone how to read. These gifts could also include connecting with teenagers easily or the ability to paint a room without error.

Let's imagine for a second that you could make money doing the three things that you love to do most, what three things would you be doing?

1. _____

2. _____

3. _____

Now that you've identified these three things, pick one of them and list three actions that you can take to accomplish your goal of earning an income doing what you love. For example, if you know that you aspire to be a professor but haven't gone to college yet, one of the first action steps that you can take is to begin looking for a college that is suitable for you. Next, set a deadline to complete the application (one week should do it).

List the three actions here:

1._____

2._____

3._____

GRATITUDE JOURNALS

Oftentimes we confuse wanting with needing and use the terms interchangeably. We *need* air to breathe. Children need to be cared for and fed. Wanting is something else. Wanting is different from needing. If you're reading this book, you most likely have a place to live, food for nourishment, and clothing to wear. What else do we need? Success is acknowledging that we already have everything that we could ever possibly need, right now.

Most great books and teachers of the world will tell you that gratitude breeds abundance. But how do we go about practicing gratitude? Although there are many ways, I've found that utilizing a gratitude journal is one of the easiest and most advantageous ways of them all.

I was introduced to gratitude journals while watching Oprah Winfrey interview Lady Gaga on one of Oprah's "I'm done hosting but I'm still the best host to ever do it so I'm going to do this other show that allows me to continue hosting" shows. These two powerful women were speaking candidly in a posh Manhattan apartment occupied by Lady Gaga's parents. A short while after seeing this episode I decided that I would create my own gratitude journal. In April of 2013, I started by recording my entries in list form. Here are my first five entries:

1. Extra soap once the big soap ran out!

2. Coupon given to me by Joyce for a free WAWA sandwich

3. Waking up today!

4. Free yoga at my job

5. Opportunity to do what I love!

As you can see, the entries that you record in your gratitude journal don't have to be life altering moments. Something as simple as receiving an unexpected phone call from a loved one or getting a great parking space at work could be included in your journal. Of course you should record the miracles, promotions, and major breakthroughs too.

I write in my gratitude journal first thing in the morning because it creates space for me to reflect on the previous days' events and think about ways that I can make the current day better than the day before. Sometimes I also write in my journal throughout the day or take it with me on vacations and long commutes. Decide for yourself what works best for you.

I've provided space for you to record your first entries until you get your own journal. If you already keep a gratitude journal, take a break from writing in your usual journal and jot down a few entries in the spaces below, just for today.

1. _____

2. _____

3. _____

4. _____

5. _____

Don't let these be your last entries. Try to incorporate this practice into your everyday life. This is one of the best and easiest ways for you to attract abundance. If you don't enjoy writing or think that you don't have the time to write in a journal, get creative. Try using the note pad on your cell phone. This might be a more manageable way for you to sustain your gratitude journal.

It's also salient to mention that writing down what you're grateful for is only the beginning. You need to *feel* grateful while you're writing in your journal. Put a smile on your face as you record your entries. If you're writing about a blessing that brought you joy and made you happy, then you need to feel that joy and happiness when you're writing in your journal. Transport yourself back to that place in your mind and really embody those feelings. This is how you emit authentic, grateful energy into the Universe so that the Universe can act like a boomerang and give you more circumstances to be grateful about.

THINK ABOUT MONEY

In his book *Think and Grow Rich*, Napoleon Hill goes into great detail about money consciousness and how to attract money into our lives. In one particular passage he explains how the acquisition of money can be compared to a river that flows in two directions. He writes: "There exists a great unseen stream of *power*, which may be compared to a river, except that it flows in two directions. One side carries all who get into that side of the stream onwards and upwards to *wealth* – and the other side flows in the opposite direction, carrying all who are unfortunate enough to get into it (and not able to extricate themselves from it) downwards to misery and poverty." Hill believes that positive thoughts place us on the side of the stream that leads to fortune, while negative thoughts do the opposite, and carry us to poverty.

Think about money. Which side of the stream are you on? Is money always coming back to you? Do you believe that you deserve more of it without any guilt associated with the thought? I'm usually on the right side of the stream, but I slip up sometimes too. For example, I catch myself unnecessarily asking how much items cost even though I know that I'm going to buy the item anyway. It's difficult to break these habits. Consistently asking about prices, checking receipts, and looking for the best bargain has the potential to place us on the wrong side of the stream. When you're on the side of the stream that is going onward and upward toward wealth, you realize that money is always coming back to you so long as you believe that it is. This doesn't mean that you live frivolously and waste money, it means that you recognize the power that you have to attract money into your life whenever you wish to.

TRAVEL: TAKE MORE TRIPS THAN YOU CAN AFFORD

Travelling is therapeutic for me. When I travel it fills me up in a way that nothing else manages to fill me up. My energy is restored and my perspective is forever changed. After taking a trip I return home having discovered unexplored parts of my personality that otherwise would've never been shown to me. I have more to write about too. We need moments in life that welcome creativity and push us out of our comfort zone the way that traveling to a place you're not familiar with does. It's been said that travel is the only thing that we pay for that makes us richer. As cliché as this sounds, it is a methodology that I subscribe to.

In the summer of 2015, I took a trip with my S.T.A.R.C.H. family to London and Paris. S.T.A.R.C.H. is a web series that documents individuals and organizations who are seeking to make the world a better place through acts of altruism and goodwill (www.starch.nyc). We were in London filming a web series episode about a robotics company in preparation for the upcoming season. Once we finished working in dreary London, we boarded a train and headed to Paris for three days. We partied with Parisians, stared in awe at the Eiffel Tower, and visited the world famous Louvre Museum. I remember getting emotional as I stood amongst the bustling crowd at the Eiffel Tower. I couldn't help but think about how mind blowing it was that I had made it all the way to Paris; me, a kid from McClellan Street in the Oakbrook Projects.

That same month I also traveled to New Orleans and Miami. I didn't necessarily have the money to do all of that traveling in one month, but I knew that these trips would enhance my life, broaden my horizons, and provide me with memories that will last a lifetime. Memories don't pay the bills though. When I returned home from Paris I was broke. I had to figure out how to attract money back into my life. I needed to generate income, share my story, and encourage other people in the process. So I wrote "Happy Broke: 5 Things To Do When Money Is Tight" and posted it on my LinkedIn page. In the article, I explore what it means to be "happy broke" and provide tips for maneuvering bouts of temporary "brokeness." Here's the article:

Is money tight for you right now? You're not alone. It's tight for me too. Working forty hours a week for someone else isn't really an option, but for the past year or so, my side hustles combined with my writing have allowed me to live comfortably. However, recent travels (that I don't regret at all) have disrupted my comfort.

But it's cool; I'm not upset about it. I'm actually excited because I know exactly what I need to do.

Here are the five actions that I am taking to maintain my happiness while I am temporarily "broke." Feel free to follow these steps if you're in the same boat.

1. Jump Into Your Passion

For me it's pretty simple, either get to work, or don't eat. This realization forces me to get on top of my game, and it should do the same for you. Reconnect with your professional network, investigate previously unexplored opportunities, and work diligently (smarter rather than harder). Maybe you're a personal trainer or an interior designer. Use this time to spruce up your website or offer a promotional deal that may increase your clientele. Or maybe you've worked a 9-5 job all of your life and haven't turned your passion into an income stream yet. This is the perfect time to begin. It all starts with a plan. Write down your goals and start planning, putting daily, weekly, and monthly time limits on each goal.

2. Believe That Money Is On Its Way

Use this down time of money flow to put your faith to work. Faith is what will keep you positive and motivated during a period that most people might perceive as a time of struggle. Then, match your faith with belief. Believe that the Universe is working in your favor to turn things around. Not only do you have to believe that your circumstances will get better, but you have to believe that they are better right now. Try your best to live in the space of knowing that everything will always be alright. This is how you create the type of life that you want for yourself – an abundant life with plenty of money to do what your heart desires.

3. Keep Your Spirit On Point

Now is the time to reconnect with your God. Try listening to Gospel music, starting something new like Thai Chi, meditation, or chanting, or increasing the number of days you practice yoga during the week. It could even be that you start reading a new daily devotional or pick up an old one that you haven't read in a while. Whatever it be, reconnect with God/the Universe/Mother Nature/your Spirit, then sit back and watch the opportunities (and money) come pouring in.

4. Help Others

If ever there was a time for you (and me) to extend a helping hand to someone, the time is now. Undoubtedly, the best way to receive more blessings in your own life is to be a blessing in someone else's life. By extending a helping hand without expecting anything in return, the Universe will repay you with opportunities and more abundance than you can imagine. Put in some hours at a local community center or connect with a young person who is looking for a mentor. The point is, help others if you want people to help you. It really is that simple.

5. Be (Extra) Grateful

Now is the time to be extra grateful. If you don't

have a gratitude journal, get one. If you have one but have not written in it in a while, crack it back open and begin jotting down all of the blessings, people, and circumstances that you can be grateful about. Wake up with gratitude in your heart and end each day focusing on those moments of gratitude. By doing this you will attract more situations to you that warrant a grateful heart.

It's easy to slip into a state of believing that you don't deserve to be in the position that you're in. When this happens you have to remind yourself of two things. 1.) This is your journey and your journey alone; a journey that has been handpicked specifically for you. Be grateful for it. 2.) There are lots of people who have it worse than you do. Remember this and give thanks for the fact that things could always be a lot worse.

This article received an outpouring of positive feedback. It connected with people because they could relate to the topic and were inspired by the message. The article also helped me to continue solidifying myself as a writer with valuable information to share with my network of social media friends and followers. As someone who is looking to be paid for a service that you provide, always brand yourself as an expert in your field, or someone who is working toward being an expert in their field. Connect with your audience by bringing them into your world and letting them be a part of your story as it is taking shape, even the not so shiny parts of your story. This is oftentimes what people gravitate toward most.

"Happy Broke" is one of the most viewed articles I've ever written. After I published it on LinkedIn it was also published on Writelaughdream.com, a website run by a talented writer out of Philadelphia named Ashley Graham. This allowed me to continue expanding my brand in a different market. If I hadn't taken those trips that subsequently put me in a temporary state of being "happy broke," these opportunities of exposure would've not been afforded to me.

Whether you decide to take three trips in one month or one really big trip per year, with so many ways to make and save money, don't let your income limit your travels. I once met a high school guidance counselor whose family prefers not to exchange Christmas gifts so that they can travel the world instead. The interior of his office looks like a museum. The walls are lined with artifacts, African masks, and pictures of him and his family on their many excursions. Remember, there are no rules mandating that you have to celebrate Christmas or any other holiday that requires you to live outside of your means and buy gifts that people probably don't need anyway.

Which three places would you visit if money was not a concern and you could go anywhere that you'd like?

1. _____

2. _____

3. _____

Here are a few ways to contribute to your travel fund and save a few bucks while traveling:

- Set aside a weekly or monthly amount that will go directly to your travel savings and then don't touch it until it's time to book your trip
- Buy plane tickets instead of Christmas gifts
- Sell anything you own that you don't absolutely love
- Consider couch surfing (www.couchsurfing.com)
- Utilize hostels
- Use a credit card that lets you accumulate frequent flyer miles
- Book a trip using your income tax return
- House sit
- Travel by bus
- Move to a place where you can earn an income teaching your native language

IT'S OKAY TO WORK FOR FREE

I felt an immense sense of gratitude as the shutters and flashes going off around me all competed for Richard Pryor's daughter's attention. It was the early evening of a pleasant spring day on 125th street in Harlem. Richard Pryor, Moms Mabley, and Redd Foxx were being inducted into the Apollo Walk of Fame. As I stood under the world famous Apollo Theater marquee amongst photographers and more seasoned journalists, I tried to appear as comfortable as possible. It was my first time covering a red carpet event. On assignment for a movie review website, I was attending the induction ceremony as a result of not being afraid to work for free.

Writing for a movie review website without being paid for it made sense for a few reasons. If I was going to the movies anyway, why not work on my craft and build up my resume by writing a story about the movie that I was seeing? By working with this website I was able to build a rapport with the owner. When he received press passes to film screenings I was someone he could ask to cover the event. This allowed me to expand my network and begin forming a relationship with the public relations person at the Apollo Theater.

No work that we ever do is for free. It doesn't matter whether you're a singer, writer, photographer, teacher, visual artist, or social media influencer, everything that you do, even if you're not being paid monetarily, will add value to your journey. I've had countless opportunities come my way because I'm not afraid to work for free and attend networking events. Just recently I collaborated with a videographer who has been helping me create some great videos. We were introduced to one another at a Thanksgiving meal organized by *The Simmons Foundation*, a philanthropic organization founded by one of my best friends and her husband. As it turned out, this videographer was looking for a way to build his portfolio and spread the word about his services, so he agreed to shoot video content for me in exchange for me helping him to promote his company, *Robert Buzzard Photography*. As creatives and forward thinking people in general, it's important to remember that money is only one form of currency. Time and service are just as valuable as money, and as our world continues to evolve, I'm sure bartering and swapping services will become more common as people begin to change the way that they look at actual value and traditional payment methods.

In *The Soul Truth* by Sheila and Marcus Gillette, the authors provide six key points to consider when manifesting abundance. I'd like to close this chapter by sharing them with you here:

1. Examine beliefs about money and worthiness.

2. Recognize your uniqueness, perfection, and divinity.

3. It is God's desire for everyone to have abundance.

4. Living a deeply spiritual, God-centered life is not in conflict with financial success; you can have it all.

5. Look to the self, not past conditioning, for the ability to receive.

6. Energy is energy. The universal energy of creation has no judgment.

Love Of Money

Chapter 6
LOVE OF GOD

Message In The Music:

"In A Sentimental Mood"
by
Duke Ellington & John Coltrane

Love
In its purest form
For sunny days
For any storm
God
You are me
And I am you
For when I love me
I love you
Love
Of
God

BELIEVE

There was always something about New York City that piqued my interest. In my early years of high school I was certain that attending New York University is what would get me to New York City. I would study journalism and create a life for myself running an urban magazine like Khadijah's character did on *Living Single*. My SAT scores didn't quite get on board with that plan though. My aspirations of living in New York would go on hiatus for a little over ten years, but the thought of walking around Time Square's neon illuminated streets in search of inspiration as yellow taxis zipped by me without worry or care stayed with me the whole time. After spending nearly thirty years in Reading, I was finally ready to make my move to New York.

"Spread love, it's the Brooklyn way" is what Biggie said. I needed to experience that. When I would visit with my friend Edna and her family, the borough felt strangely familiar. I loved the fact that at any given time I could hear one of Jay-Z's hits blasting out of the speakers of a car passing by. And whenever the savory aromas of well-seasoned Caribbean food enveloped my nostrils it brought a smile to my face and reminded me of home. The people were beautiful too, and uniquely stylish. The culture and the energy were overflowing, and I wanted to dive in head first and immerse myself in its authenticity.

To make my dream of moving to Brooklyn a reality I wrote down exactly what I wanted on a post-it note. "I am a successful writer living in Reading, Pa and Brooklyn, New York" I scribbled neatly onto the pink square. I looked at it daily and focused my energy on manifesting what I'd written down. But more importantly, I believed that it could happen. I didn't want to give up my hometown; I wanted to live in both cities. I knew that what I would learn in New York was valuable to the work that I did in Reading. I also knew that it was possible. I didn't know anyone who was living in two cities at once, and it definitely wasn't the norm, but to me, this didn't make it any less possible. So I got busy. The first thing that I needed to do was find a job and a home in New York.

With some luck and persistence I landed a job at Wood Tobe-Coburn College in Manhattan. I didn't have a place to live yet but I accepted that job because I knew that the Universe would work out the rest of the details for me. For three months I commuted six hours round-trip from Pennsylvania to New York. The commute wasn't ideal but the job was perfect. There was lots of flexibility and I was allowed to set my own schedule. My position as an admissions rep and workshop facilitator allowed me to explore my new city and practice my public speaking skills too. My job provided the opportunity to travel throughout the five boroughs facilitating career awareness workshops for high school students.

When I wasn't working I attended events and tried to meet as many people as possible. From open mic nights at *Shrine* in Harlem, to chillin' on the boulder size rocks in Central Park with my friend Coby, I was a sponge and New York City was a thick liquid that I soaked up religiously. I continued to write too. I took on a number of different freelance positions, sometimes writing restaurant reviews and other times writing about hip hop culture and the people who govern it.

After commuting back and forth to Pennsylvania and occasionally crashing on my friend Rochelle's couch, without a broker, application fee, or credit check, I found a place to live in Washington Heights, one of the most vibrant and culturally rich communities in Manhattan. I got lucky. My childhood friend Ashlee was preparing to make the move from Reading to New York and the apartment that she was moving into had a spare room for rent. It wasn't Brooklyn but I was excited to officially move to the big apple. For the next year and a half I lived on 179th street, up the block from the A train and across the street from the massive George Washington Bridge.

Then, without notice or a real explanation as to why, I got kicked out of my apartment and was given thirty days to find a new place to live. That night, after being asked to leave the place that was finally starting to feel like home, I began searching for a new one. I texted everyone I knew in New York. One of the first people I texted was a singer, songwriter, and proud Brooklyn native named Cole. I befriended Cole after writing about her performance at the *Blue Note Jazz Club* in Manhattan a few years before I moved to New York. As fate would have it, she was about to go on tour and needed someone to take over her lease. The rent would be the exact same amount that I was paying in Manhattan. That was all I needed to hear. I was in.

Before I knew it I was a Brooklyn resident living in a brownstone on Monroe Street in Bed Stuy, a neighborhood that up until then, I only saw come to life through the eyes of Chris Rock on *Everybody Hates Chris*. With its tree-lined streets and innate prestige, sections of my new neighborhood reminded me of the block that the Huxtables made famous on *The Cosby Show*.

I remember my move to Brooklyn clearly. It was a cold winter day and it was snowing. I'm sure my friend Rony remembers it too. He was a trooper, he never complained once and refused to let me pay him for helping me move. After moving all of my things into my new room, I was pleasantly surprised to find four crystals resting comfortably on my windowsill. Two of the crystals were a violet color and two were light pink. As I picked up one of each color and felt their energy pulsate in my palm, I wondered if Cole forgot them there or left them on purpose. I wasn't sure. I was sure of one thing though, all was well. I knew everything would be fine when I found a new apartment so quickly, but my new crystal roommates were a much appreciated confirmation. Then a few hours later, it hit me. What I wrote down on that pink post-it note became my reality. I was living in Reading and Brooklyn. The route that I took to get to Brooklyn wasn't planned, but the end result was exactly what it was supposed to be.

Many of us don't realize how powerful we are. Our thoughts and intentions create our lives. Whatever we believe to be true about ourselves will be true. In religion we often hear the word faith. Believing is having faith. What we believe to be true about ourselves has a major impact on our lives. Think about that. I may not be a *New York Times* Best-Selling author yet, but I believe myself to be one. I also believe myself to be a world traveler and a known speaker and philanthropist.

What do you believe yourself to be? Use the spaces below to write down what you believe yourself to be:

1. _____

2. _____

3. _____

Forming the idea in your mind is the first step. Then you have to write it down. If you're not sure what to write in those spaces, sitting in silent meditation will help you find the answers. You might find them quickly or it could take months or even years, so be patient and kind to yourself while you wait. In the meantime, start doing more of what you love and less of what you don't.

*****

Every year a local magazine dedicates one of their issues to recognizing the best the county has to offer. A freelance writer. A photographer. A coffee shop. Best of Berks. Voting is done online. Early on in my career and still wet behind the ears as a writer, I decided to throw myself in the running for the title of *Favorite Freelance Writer*. I sent the link to vote for me to a few of my family members and friends and posted it on my Facebook page. Then I thought, "What if I win? Am I actually the best freelance writer in my county?" Hell no! I wasn't the favorite in the county, maybe the favorite on my block, but the favorite in the county, *nah*, that wasn't me. I came to this realization quickly and didn't like the way it felt, so I made the decision to start living as if I was the best writer in my county. I began seeking out opportunities to write regularly and started to build my portfolio. I attended events and wrote about them without being paid to do it, and I finally began calling myself a writer. One month later I landed a freelance editing gig and began writing for a local website. Securing these two jobs didn't make me the best writer in my county, but it did motivate me to work toward one day being recognized as the best (The funny and ironic thing about this story is that there was no way for me to win the contest anyway. A few weeks after soliciting votes I learned that only freelance writers who contributed to a certain Berks County themed publication were eligible to receive the recognition).

In order to accomplish any goal you have to first believe that it can happen, then match that belief with hard work and persistence. The Universe will take care of the rest. It may arrive somewhat differently than you had planned. And it may take a while and you will have to overcome obstacles that make you question why you've started to begin with, but the truth is nothing beats God, belief, and hard work.

What can you believe into existence right now?

I will _____

In order to do this, I will work hard at:

_____

> *"Come on now, who do you*
> *Who do you, who do you*
> *Who do you think you are?*
> *Ha ha ha, bless your soul*
> *You really think you're in control?"*
> – Gnarls Barkley

LET GO OF CONTROL & EXPECTATIONS

We begin the same way every Monday, with a four minute meditation. Then the floor is opened up for a conversation about all things spiritual. It's how we hold the space. During this week's *Holding The Space* meeting, Diane (spiritual counselor and host) said something that resonated with me. She said: "if my life were a sentence, I'm trying to live it without periods." Her bold statement made me sit up in my chair. "Do I live my life without periods?," I asked myself. "For the most part I do," I retorted to my conscious.

What I took away from Diane's statement and my analysis of it, is that when we live a life with periods we discount the power of divine order. When we live a life without periods we give up control and begin trusting our journey and the Source that is guiding it. Living this way detaches us from the disappointment that arises when situations don't work out in our favor. Trusting divine order and working with it, not against it or without it, is how we exercise our Love Of God. Learning to let go of control and expectations so that I can trust the process has been one of the most rewarding and difficult lessons for me to learn. It takes practice.

*****

It was day one of 2017, New Year's Day. There was so much that I wanted to do. I needed to clean and sage my apartment, get organized, write down my goals for the new year, and meditate. But none of that happened. Instead, I laid in bed for hours. My body and spirit needed rest, so I rested. It was great. I remained nestled in the comfort of my comforter until noon. I watched a movie and read one or two articles on my phone.

I did one load of wash and one other menial house chore. That's it.

The first few days of the new year got off to a slow start for me. It was the perfect way to practice letting go of expectations. As Oprah likes to call it, I was in the "flow." I was taking each moment as it came without worrying about the past or the future. The present was all that mattered. By the second week of the new year I was rested and reenergized. I booked a speaking gig the following week and was back to being just as productive as I had been during the weeks leading up to the new year.

*****

At the end of that same month I attended a writing retreat in Costa Rica at Norma's Villas (www.normasvillas.com), a family-run resort that I called home for nine perfect days. I arrived in alluring Costa Rica on an almost uncomfortably warm Friday evening as a bright orange sun was beginning to make way for a pale moon. After touring the premises and taking a quick trip to a food stand not far from the villas, I was ready to relax. I was tired so I didn't do much work that first night. I got myself acclimated to my new space and made some progress on a newspaper article that I needed to submit to my editor that coming Sunday. Saturday came and went. It was a productive day but I hadn't worked on this book at all. I attended two informative self-publishing workshops, took a nap (which I never do), swam, and meditated while surrounded by a breathtakingly green Costa Rican backdrop.

It was Sunday morning and I had just finished eating breakfast, which I'm sure included rice of some sort. Rice is served with every meal in Costa Rica. Gallo pinto is the "breakfast rice" that we ate on most mornings, alongside eggs, and the freshest and sweetest mangoes I've ever eaten. After breakfast I planned to sit outside and soak up the sun while finishing my article. Once my article was finished I could move on to getting serious book writing done. The purpose for coming to the writing retreat was to make significant progress on this book, so my expectations were high.

The sun was shining and my coffee was working as I made myself comfortable on the small porch outside of my villa. After securing my computer in my lap and my cell phone beside me, I was ready to get busy. Then my cell phone almost fell on the hard concrete. I was so worried about my distraction device breaking that I forgot about the laptop in my lap and the coffee in my left hand. I saved my phone to the detriment of my computer, which now had drops of coffee spilled on its black keys.

"No worries," I thought to myself. "My phone is good and there's only a small amount of coffee resting on a handful of letters in the center of the keyboard." Little did I know that was all it would take to put my laptop out of commission. I cautiously removed the drops of coffee, but none of the keys on my keyboard worked. I couldn't believe it. I had flown all the way to Costa Rica expecting to get four chapters of my book finished, and now my laptop wasn't working at all. I quickly removed the battery from my computer and did everything that Google told me to do. I was upset but I needed to focus on finding a printer so that I could print out the draft to the article that I had been working on that was due in less than twenty-four hours. I had to make final revisions and send it to my editor before my deadline. After figuring out where I could print my article draft, I caught a ride with a fellow writer named Steven to Turucarres. Shortly, we were in a quaint and colorful little town about twenty minutes from the resort. Now I needed to find a printer. After a little searching and putting my broken and limited Spanish to use, I found a store where I could print a copy of my draft and begin editing. I was still bothered by the thought of not being able to use my laptop, but I was determined to make a positive out of the situation. After editing my article draft, I wrote a journal entry while sitting on the side of the road under the comforting arms of a small tree:

"It's day 2 of my Costa Rica trip. I've been wanting to write a journal entry and now that my computer isn't working right I am kind of forced to. That's a good thing though. I'm trying to figure out why God/the Universe would play this trick on me (lol). I feel like I already kind of know the answer. I am very distracted by my phone

these days. Because of that I spilled coffee on my keyboard and now it won't work properly. I planned to get a lot of writing for my book done but I guess God had other plans, unless it starts working sometime soon. I told myself this morning that I need to turn my phone off for the day and just focus on myself and my writing, but I didn't listen to myself/God. Another lesson. I'm still in good spirits for the most part but, shit, did the lesson have to come now? I'm believing that my computer will work again. Maybe later or maybe tomorrow. Either way I can't complain, Costa Rica is beautiful! I've done yoga twice, swam, and had two good self-publishing workshops surrounded by palm trees and greenery. I'm going to do more swimming and more meditating. Worst case scenario I won't be able to do much writing with my computer until this time next week when I can hopefully use Demetrius's computer when we meet in Miami. I'm thinking that I can do some writing for the book by hand. This is better than not writing at all. Maybe my writing by hand will give me some insight that using a keyboard won't. I already feel a little better by putting these words on paper. I always do. I'm starting to get a little emotional now just thinking about my gift and my challenges and journey. Crying on the side of the road sitting under a tree was not in my Costa Rican plans. Recently I've been learning to let go of expectations, but I guess not all the way because I was expecting to get a lot of work done on my book during this trip."

After editing and journaling I made my way back to the store where I printed my draft so that I could make the corrections to my article and e-mail it to my editor. Now I was ready to make my trek back to Norma's Villas. I had three choices. I could wait for and try my best to navigate the bus system using the fifty or so Spanish words in my vocabulary, order an Uber, or take a ninety minute walk.

With two ripe bananas and a half full bottle of water, I decided to walk back. I figured this would be the best way to relieve some stress and immerse myself in Costa Rica's grandeur. During my walk I couldn't help but to capture all of the colors around me, both with my mind and with my cell phone camera – the rich turquoises and bright yellows that adorned the homes gave me no other choice but to give them my undivided attention.

The walk was long but it was one of the most alluring and much needed walks I've ever taken. When I finally arrived back at Norma's Villas I was exhausted and sweaty but I immediately changed into my swimsuit so that I could go for a swim. By now I was fully accepting of what happened to my computer. I believed that it would work again before the retreat was over, but I let go of the expectation of it doing so because I accepted that it was out of my control. Once I got to the pool I began writing in my journal again:

"It's a few hours later and I've fully accepted that I may or may not have a working computer for the week

and I'm okay with it, it's out of my hands; not all the way though. I know that there's a greater chance of it working if I believe that it will, but despite that, it's all good either way. I'm in Costa Rica, and as they say – Pura Vida!"

After journaling I meditated in the baby pool. With my long lanky legs crossed Indian style in the shallow water, and my eyes closed, I probably looked crazy to the other swimmers, but I didn't care. I sat there for a good twenty minutes reveling in feelings of fullness, warmth, and love. Omnipresent peace. It was just what I needed after the day that I had. During my meditation the Universe reminded me that it would always be on my side despite any barriers that may be thrown my way. I was reassured, yet again, that there's always light at the end of whatever our human minds perceive as a dark tunnel.

By the time I opened my eyes to bring the meditation to a close I was all the way good. The walk, the journaling, and the stillness helped me to see that what started out to be my worse day in Costa Rica was actually my best day. What I took away from that experience is that as much as I would like to think that I'm in control, I'm not, and that's okay. That night before I went to bed my laptop was back to working normally again.

FORGET ABOUT GETTING A LOT DONE

One night in a sweaty Bikram yoga class, I decided that I would no longer aim to get "a lot" of work done. While in the middle of some pose, I decided that by expecting to get "a lot" done we place unrealistic expectations on ourselves and measure our worth by how productive we are or aren't. By making plans to get "a lot" done you're telling the Universe that you're in control. Control shouldn't be what we're after. We benefit when we're more concerned with our intention than we are with our productivity. When we work purposefully with the intent to do our best we will always be happy with the outcome of our work. This doesn't mean that we shouldn't hold ourselves accountable though. You know when you're working purposefully and with the best intention, and you know when you're doing something with half commitment too.

When you value your work (even if you're not at the point where you're doing something that you love) you won't have any problems giving it the respect that it deserves, and as a result of that, you always get "a lot" done. But again, try not to get too caught up in the amount of work that you're getting done because this leaves the door open for judgement to be brought into the equation. It's easy to get down on ourselves when there's judgment involved, but when you're doing your life's work, there's no room for judgement, just keep doing the work at a pace that's comfortable for you.

The best thing about doing our life's work is that when we are doing this work we will always be getting "a lot" done because we've figured out how to seamlessly weave this work into our daily lives. This is where the magic happens – when every encounter, TV show, joke, song, or conversation can be used as inspiration for the work that you're doing. If you've reached this point in your journey, take advantage of it and be grateful for it. If you're not quite there yet keep figuring out ways to initiate this type of creativity in your life. Before you know it you'll be getting "a lot" done without considering time or ever thinking twice about it.

KNOW WHO GOD IS FOR YOU

It's the equivalent to watching *Martin* reruns with Kevin Hart and Dave Chappelle as they compete to tell you a joke. In other words, it's hilarious when people ask me if I believe in God. I can't begin to tell you how many times I've been asked about whether or not I believe in God because of my views on church and religion. The truth is I couldn't live the life that I live without believing in a Source that is much more powerful and perfect than I am. It just wouldn't work. I've turned down well-paying full-time jobs, gone without electricity for a summer, and survived off of $1 slices of pizza in New York City because I never stopped believing in God and I knew that God had my back and that better days were ahead.

God is love, an energy, not a man or a woman, both masculine and feminine, and not something to be praised – celebrated – yes, but praised, no (as humans we want praise, the energy that is God does not need our praise). Once you know who God is for you and what God means to you, it will be a lot harder for people to project their opinions and misconceptions about your relationship with God onto you. Stand firm in your truth and remind yourself of it every day by engaging in activities that reinforce God's presence in your life. Nurture and love this presence because it is the nucleus of the relationship with self. This relationship is undoubtedly the most fruitful relationship that you will ever have.

FINAL THOUGHTS ON GOD
& DOING GOD'S WORK

There's a higher power that wants you to use your gifts to make the world a better place. When you work in conjunction with this higher power, whatever you choose to call it, life will begin to unfold for you in new and exciting ways. It won't be easy though. Making a life for yourself doing what you love might be one of the most difficult things you will ever do, especially if what you love involves being an entrepreneur. In fact, I can only imagine that raising children is a more draining and overwhelming experience. But, pursuing your dreams doesn't have to be draining and overwhelming. When you trust the process and the divine order of your life you realize that what is for you is for you and what is not just isn't.

In order to stay motivated we have to remember that when we're following our dreams, we're doing God's work. Feeling overwhelmed and drained should only be temporary. If we are constantly tired and overwhelmed we're doing too much chasing and not enough believing. The present moment is all that exists. When we are living in that moment and making our best attempt at putting love at the forefront of everything that we do, there is no need to chase anything, not even happiness. The pursuit of happiness can make you unhappy. Be happy, pursue nothing. When we are happy all that we want and need will pursue us. Love.

MAKE LOVE YOUR RELIGION
SOUNDTRACK

1. *What's Going On* by Marvin Gaye

2. *Blessed* by Jill Scott

3. *One* by Mary J. Blige, featuring U2

4. *I N I* by Amel Larrieux

5. *Give 'em Hell* by Talib Kweli

6. *America* by Nas

7. *Vivir Mi Vida* by Marc Anthony

8. *Juicy* by Notorious B.I.G.

9. *Curry Chicken* by Joey Bada$$

10. *In A Sentimental Mood* by John Coltrane and Duke Ellington

11. *Crazy* by Gnarls Barkley

11.04.2020 1424